THE BEGINNER'S GUIDE TO YOUTUBE ADVERTISING

DISCOVER THE VIDEO CONTENT MARKETING SECRETS AND HOW TO START A YOUTUBE CHANNEL FOR BUSINESS

LAWRENCE GIBSON

CONTENTS

INTRODUCTION

Perhaps everyone—you, your mom, your dad, your neighbor, your neighbor's workmate—know who Justin Bieber is. With more than 60 million likes on his Facebook page, almost 50 million followers on Twitter, and about 8 million subscribers on YouTube, there is no denying that Bieber is one of the most celebrated people in Hollywood.

Back in early 2007, a twelve-year-old kid whose username was "Kidrauhl" started posting song covers on YouTube. Of course, at first, he still didn't have many views. "It had a hundred views, then a thousand views, then ten thousand views…" That kid was none other than Justin Bieber. After a while, he got discovered by his manager who then sent him to Usher, and the rest is history.

Unlike other Hollywood personalities who have the blood of celebrities running through their veins, Justin used to be just like you and me, a simple person who dreamed of making it big someday. For that matter, YouTube has been his steppingstone to make his dream turn into a reality.

Just like Bieber, you too can make use of YouTube as a tool for making it big on your chosen career, be it in performing, or even in your business. But first of all, let us first discuss the basics of YouTube.

What is YouTube?

YouTube, just like Facebook and Twitter, is a form of social media. However, its difference among other social media is that it specializes on video hosting and sharing.

YouTube is a platform that enables video sharing to inform, entertain, inspire and educate. Three former PayPal employees Steve Chen, Chad Hurley, and Jared Karim founded YouTube in year 2005, and then Google bought it a year after.

Since its introduction, YouTube has undeniably been a huge success. Cofounder Steve Chen told Business Week two years after YouTube's foundation that they owe their company's accomplishment to the emergence and availability of affordable video cameras, the growth of fiber optic lines from 1999 to 2004, and the increasing number of people with access to

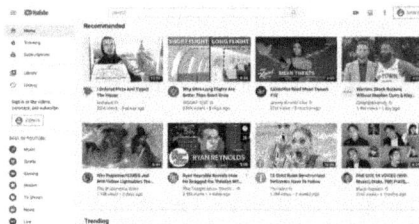

broadband internet.

YouTube has a simple yet inviting interface. "The coolness is in the content, not the interface." Once you enter www.youtube.com on your browser's tab, you will be presented with its homepage. Here is how YouTube's Homepage looks like.

YouTube's homepage already has practically everything you need to use on this site. There are the Search bar where you can just type any video you would want to watch, the Sign in button for you to log into your account and upload a video, like other videos and interact with other YouTube users, the Upload button for you to share your own video to YouTube (what's the essence of creating a channel on YouTube if you are not going to upload a video, anyway?), and the videos that have the most views or are highly recommended for you. YouTube is not that complicated after all, is it?

What Makes YouTube Different

In the expanse of the Internet universe, YouTube is not—definitely not —the only video-hosting site that is available to the people. There are still lots of other websites that offers video sharing services. But what makes YouTube stand out among the rest? One reason is because YouTube tops the ranking in Google search results. Has there been an incident when you search on Google "One Direction Story of my Life music video" but YouTube is not on the top results? Chances are if you search for any kind of video online, the top result will almost always be on YouTube.

That is one of the reasons why a huge wave of people is being drawn to YouTube each and every day. YouTube tops the Google search result, which means YouTube will be the first site that people will see and visit.

Another reason is that it can handle a lot of people every day for it has a great (great is probably an understatement) traffic source. As of today, statistics shows that YouTube caters to a billion people every day. Just imagine how large that number is? Just put it this way: If you're on your computer and billions of people keep on sending you requests to access your computer, what would that be like? Being a huge company, YouTube can accommodate a large number of people which means there is no hassle with regards to traffic and access.

Moreover, YouTube is convenient to use. Its features can easily be seen on its Homepage, which makes it hassle-free, even if it's your first time to visit the site.

What's in the bank?

YouTube is a home for thousands or even millions of videos from everyone around the world. Because the number of videos that can be found on this site is quite unimaginable already, it's somehow impossible to come up with concrete classifications of what videos are usually found on YouTube. Nonetheless, YouTube places different videos into categories (which can also be found on their Homepage) which just makes searching for videos easier for us.

Entertainment. Most of the time, people go to YouTube to be entertained. They want to listen to music or watch music videos or movie trailers. Some people also upload TV show episodes for those who would want to catch up or even movies that they have. Some even make their own "show" and entertain the viewers.

Comedy. Just like entertainment, some people go to YouTube to get some fair dose of laughter and happiness. Whether it's as random as a person who tripped over or a rooster that laughs like a human, people will surely want to watch those videos, making Comedy as one of the most popular categories on YouTube.

Pets and Animals. While some want to entertain people, some just want to share how cute, fluffy, and adorable their pets are. Though it can be an entertainment to some point, the Pets and Animals categories are specially made for videos that star nothing but our animal best friends. If you are a big pet lover, then this category is surely for you.

Travel and Places. For those who would like to explore different places but rather are just snuggled up in their couches or beds, then this category is probably the answer to your dreams. Under this one, you would find videos created by people who have gone to vacations to different places and would like to share their experience and how great those places were.

These are just some of the categories to give you an overview what can normally be found on YouTube and might as well give you some ideas on how to start creating videos and what your videos must contain.

WHY YOU SHOULD BE MARKETING ON YOUTUBE

To make the right decision and have a positive influence on your business, it is worth taking a look at some of the benefits of marketing your business on YouTube. Far from what the numbers tell us about YouTube, there are other advantages that your business would gain by using it.

YouTube is Free

One of the most interesting facts about YouTube is that it is a free platform. You need not pay for anything as you market your brand. This is a benefit that you wouldn't want to pass on. If you have been using conventional methods to market your business, then you must be aware of how costly it can get. Marketing is never cheap. Getting people to fall in love with your brand might take years. Big market players understand the importance of marketing. As such, they would do anything just to ensure that they take advantage of free marketing platforms such as YouTube.

The process of creating your business channel won't take a lot of time. You only need to create a Google account, and in minutes you can have your business channel up and running. However, there are a few

1

things here and there that you will need. For example, you will need a good camera for video creation. Also, there are video editing tools that you will need. These tools will guarantee that you upload quality videos.

You will also have to spend money on making sure that quality content is posted to your business page. Yes, YouTube is free. Nonetheless, it doesn't mean that you will not be spending anything completely. If possible, you have to find an expert to help you in creating highly engaging content. This is one thing that should be made clear in your mind.

YouTube Is Constantly Growing

Just like any other social media page, YouTube is constantly growing. This growth is influenced by the fact that people accessing the internet also grow on a daily basis. As people move from conventional ways of doing this, the world of the internet also grows. Therefore, there is a possibility that there would be more people accessing YouTube the following year.

Consider the common problems that you face when using products or relying on services from companies out there. Often, people seek solutions without having to call their friends or relatives. They do this by using YouTube. If they get stuck in assembling their furniture, the first thing that comes to mind is YouTube. It has all the answers.

YouTube also offers solutions to life problems that you might be going through. There are tons of motivational videos that you can turn to. These videos are accessed free of charge. You don't have to pay for anything to watch motivational videos that could transform your life. The main point here is that YouTube presents itself as a platform where anything could be posted. People find their solutions on YouTube.

In relation to the above, if your product promises to solve a certain problem, then YouTube would be a great place to market it. The platform is promising. The numbers tell it all. With the possibility of more people accessing the platform in years to come, it means that it is a platform worth investing in.

Have you thought of the fact that it is easily accessed anywhere in the world? Therefore, there are no geographical boundaries that will limit your followers. What does this mean? Your company has the opportunity of expanding its operations globally. Don't forget the fact that you will not have to spend a lot to achieve this.

A graphical analysis shown reveals the fact that the number of YouTubers will continue to grow in the coming years. This is good news for businesses that will be using the platform to market their brands. Your business should also turn to YouTube considering the potential benefits that could come its way. A motivational factor that should push you to invest in the platform is the fact that you don't pay for anything. It is a free platform. Your marketing strategies will take you to the top of your rivals in the same market.

Showcasing Your Products/Services

As we continue unfolding more on the importance of marketing your product/service on YouTube, content is an area that we will discuss in depth. In as much as internet users kill time using social media pages, it doesn't mean that your content should be compromised. Content is what will differentiate you from other companies selling their products and services through YouTube.

The advantage you gain by using YouTube to market your brand is that you get to showcase to the world what your brand is all about. YouTube is all about videos. Certainly, this is what most socialites are after. Videos have become the best form of entertainment. Also, companies have realized that videos are the best ways of sending promotional messages. This is because they are highly engaging.

Prove this by scrolling any social media page. Most content posted therein are videos. Videos are more engaging as compared to other forms of posts. They are not only entertaining, but they are also informative. With the high engagement rate that you will be getting in using videos, you can be sure that you will get more people viewing your brand.

The videos that you post will inform and entertain your audience. They will know how to use your product. Moreover, the posts will also help them in understanding the benefits they could gain in using your product/service. Using demonstrational videos builds trust in the minds of your target market. They will garner an understanding that your product or service will offer a solution to the problem that they might have been facing.

It is important to note that your audience will not solely use YouTube to know more about your company. The platform will make it easy for you to inform your followers about the existence of your business website. Therefore, traffic to your website can be driven through YouTube. This way, you get more followers to your business home page. The benefit gained here is that people would be more aware of what your brand is all about. To achieve this, you need to make good use of call to action messages.

Building Awareness and Trustworthiness

A major challenge that most businesses face today is connecting with the prospects on a personal level. Consumers depending on brands aim to be more aware of what they are about to depend on. Therefore, they strive to gain information before choosing to settle for any brand. By keeping this in mind, you will better understand what consumers expect from your company. Consumers have the power to make their choices. They could choose you or simply opt for rival brands in the market. However, if your brand sells out as a trustworthy brand, then most likely they would be choosing you.

YouTube creates awareness to people about what you are selling. How is this possible? When one individual comes across your post, they would want to know whether your product fits their needs. Once they realize that your product is promising, they will share your video with their friends on social media. The promotional message will continue to be shared in other social media pages until it goes viral. Well, this is how awareness is created. But, before your content is shared, it has to be engaging and unique. It has to sweep your audience off their feet. To achieve this, you have to invest in hiring an expert to help you in creating winning videos.

Depending on what you are selling, you should understand that your followers seek trust. They yearn to depend on a brand that they can trust. So, can they trust your company to deliver? Can they be certain that your company will not disappoint them? Well, you have to convince them that you can meet their demands. Your convincing power will be reflected through the promotional videos that you will be sharing. This shows you that the quality of your videos matters a lot.

If it is services that you are selling, YouTube will give you an excellent platform to showcase what you have. This is a page where you build credibility about your brand. You are here to convince your potential followers that you are the best in the market. Give them advice where possible. Show them how best they can use the product you are offering. Ultimately, they will appreciate the convenience that they gain in using your product.

Get More Subscribers

Another benefit that your business will gain from using YouTube is getting more subscribers. These are the people that find your videos interesting and would want to know more about your company. If you keep posting highly engaging content, you can rest assured that you will have many followers subscribing to your business channel. Well, this will not happen automatically without their knowledge. You have to motivate your audience to subscribe. There should be a call to action message reminding your audience that they should subscribe after watching the promotional video.

A high subscription rate will mean that your brand is doing well with regards to your marketing campaign. It will be of great advantage to your business as your followers will be notified by YouTube about your new posts. Therefore, you will never worry about informing your audience that there are new products that you have introduced in the market.

Solve Customer Problems

There is a certainty that there are some customers that might find issues while dealing with your product. This implies that they would want answers to solve their problems. Finding these answers conveniently is the only way that they will be motivated to keep using your brand. So, YouTube gives you the benefit of answering your customer queries with ease. All you need is quality tutorial videos. These videos will guide you in ensuring that your customers solve their problems conveniently.

With the benefits that will be coming your way as you use YouTube for your business's marketing demand, there is a need for you to invest in the platform. You will not only grow your business with time, but you will also save a lot in getting followers to depend on your brand. Far from the fact that you will spend nothing on marketing your brand on this platform, the convenience that you will be getting all round should be a convincing reason for you to think about adding it to your social media marketing strategy.

Research and Competition Analysis

Finding out more about your competitors will help you with your campaign for content marketing. Although this shouldn't get in the way of your creative ideas, analyzing your competitors will help you find out what works, along with tactics to help your viewers feel more interested and engaged in your channel. The best tool for this is the YouTube Analysis feature on BirdSong Analytics. This tool allows you to pay as you go. It only requires a channel name to use, and this handy tool will give you lots of useful reports and stats, such as:

• Your competitor's channel's best upload time (in terms of getting likes).

• The ideal day to upload for getting likes, according to your competitor.

• When you should upload to receive audience comments, according to the competition.

• The best day to upload videos in order to get comments, according to your competition's channel.

• The way the length of your videos can impact viewing figures.

• The way the length of the videos can impact viewer engagement.

• Commonly used terms in video captions, and more.

It also allows you to download a spreadsheet from Excel that lists all of the videos from your competitors, including upload date, description, title, duration, and day of upload, along with how many views, comments, and likes each video has. Mess around with conditional formatting and filters within the spreadsheet, and you can learn even more about competitor tactics. Make sure that you look into more than one channel before attempting to use these reports for your video creation.

CREATING AND OPTIMIZING YOUR CHANNEL

Setting Up Your YouTube Channel

Set up your YouTube Channel when you set up the rest of your social media profiles. Even if you are months away from posting videos! Put links to your YouTube channel on your website and social media profiles to get people subscribing to your channel before you post a single video. This will get people excited about seeing more from you and help you start creating a community while you're building your strong foundation!

A. Choosing a Name: This should be the same as your website address/name. Make it easy to remember, short, catchy and easy to spell.

B. Channel Description: Review your Brand, Purpose, Target Audience and Difference, then write a bio for the "About/Description" of your YouTube channel based on that information. Your description should tell a story: who you are, why you're making videos, why your target audience would want to watch and what they will get out of watching. People like to watch, follow and engage with other people. Make your description personal — and make it real. Don't forget to include your key words!

C. Header Image: Your header image should represent who you are, what your channel is about and your purpose. Make it interesting and eye catching, and make it stand out. A bold, clean image will cause viewers to pause and want to learn more. Make sure it's high quality. If you can't create a high-quality header image yourself, hire someone! (Check out Fiverr or Thumbtack.)

D. Your Channel Icon: People are drawn to people, especially faces. Putting your picture in your header image is optional, but it's NOT optional in your Icon. Your icon represents you in the YouTube universe. People connect with people, not logos, vans, RVs, scenes, clip art or even pets. Your channel Icon needs to be a picture of you (you can include your pet). Get a quality photo of yourself in a setting that portrays what your channel is about and use it across all your social media.

E. Put links to your website in your channel description: Once you monetize your website with affiliate ads, visits matter. Always make it easy for your audience to visit your website

F. Add Social Media links to your header: When you create/edit your header image on YouTube, you are given the option to add links to your social media profiles. Add these to help your audience find you.

Optimizing your Set-up on YouTube

For you to attract audience to your YouTube channel, you must learn how to optimize your setup. Since there are millions of other YouTube accounts out there, make sure that yours will stand out among the rest.

Brafton, a content marketing agency that helps online businesses, created a list of ways on how you can optimize your YouTube setup.

1. Channel setup and design. You must create a positive look on your channel to attract your audience. Make sure to put your business logo,

the links to your website and other social media accounts, your profile information, and keyword tags to make your account appear to search results.

2. Video content strategy. Come up with different video ideas that are uniquely yours to be able to reach a lot of audiences and will boost your sales.

3. Calls to action. Make sure that your viewers won't just stay on their couches after seeing your video. Put your call-to-action (CTA) on your YouTube page, within the video itself, and to the video description.

4. Annotations. "Make sure your main points are clear with interactive commentary," writes Brafton. Annotations add background information, CTA, and links to other related videos, on your videos itself.

5. Thumbnails. Thumbnails also affect one's judgments with regards to choosing which video to watch. Generate one that will stand out among the rest.

6. Search friendly video tags. Use relevant tags for your videos so that it will be easier for your videos to appear on search results.

7. Playlist. Make use of YouTube's playlist feature to increase your viewer's engagement to your channel and videos.

8. Engage. Be accessible to your audience as much as possible and communicate with them all the time. Update your channel as often as you can and answer your viewer's inquiries and comments.

9. Subscriptions, social, and cross promotion. Subscribe to other accounts as well so that people can notice you more. Make use of those share buttons as well, which will post a link to your Facebook, Twitter, and other accounts.

10. Analyze insights. "Be a smart director," writes Brafton. Monitor your viewership, subscriptions, and engagements for this will refine your video strategies.

UNDERSTAND YOUR AUDIENCE

The first step in planning for a great video to create is probably the identification of your target market. Do you want to attract kids because your business products are made for kids? Do you want to invite mothers to buy your products using your videos?

The way on how you would make your videos as well as the treatment that you are going to use in making your videos are largely dependent on your audience. Of course, the approach that you will be using for kids is a lot different as compared to that which you will use for adults. So, it is important to have a clear idea on who you are targeting to be your viewers.

Who is your customer?

The people you are trying to reach are another factor in determining whether YouTube blends into your plans. Who are you selling to - and why?

This is Marketing 101 principle, so if I state the obvious, forgive me. But many advertisers, particularly those who work online, either does not know the basics or overtime, sometimes, neglect them. The most important thing you can do is to say the obvious at times.

All the ads should be about the client, so you need to learn who that consumer is and what he needs. Go through the guide below to decide who you should work on:

- How old is your primary client?
- Is it a male or female customer?
- Are your customers married, or are they single?
- What is the average annual income of your customers?
- Where are your clients living?
- Where do you shop with your customer?
- What does your client like to do in their spare time?
- How does it represent the client or herself?
- How do you prefer to receive details from your client: through newspaper, television, radio or the Internet?
- What domains are your clients often using?
- How does your client reach the Internet — through a computer or mobile device, and at what level of connection?
- Which items are your clients using at the moment?
- Is your target customer a new user or someone who doesn't use the commodity yet?
- Does your client know your company or your product?
- If so, what does your client think of your business and your services—what is his impression of you?

These are just a couple of things you need to know about your target company. For example, the more you learn, the more you will meet the desires and expectations of the client. The less you know, the more in the dark, you guess — and guessing in the dark is a very unsuccessful and wasteful way of creating a marketing plan. For example, another collection of relevant questions to ask applies to YouTube itself in terms of integrating YouTube into your marketing mix. Does your customer access the YouTube site? If so, how frequently? Why is he accessing the website? What does YouTube think of him? Which sorts of things does he enjoy watching? How does He feel about YouTube's "business" videos? If your client is an active YouTube user, and his content is accessible to commercial messages, YouTube holds promise as a marketing tool for your business. On the other extreme, if your client rarely uses YouTube, or is opposed to corporate ads intruding into his content, you really shouldn't have YouTube in your marketing mix. After all, you do not want to market if the client's not.

Know what your audience wants

Since you are dependent on your viewers and you want to attract them to be your potential clients for your business, then it is important to know what they want or what their interests are.

If you are targeting kids, then most probably your videos will contain characters or elements that kids love to watch. You can make use of cartoon characters to attract the attention of these kids. On the other hand, if you want to attract adults, then your approach will be different. If your target viewers are, say, mothers, then you should appeal to their interests as well as their needs and their family's needs.

Know what your videos must contain

As you create your video, always keep in mind your goal: to make profit. But even though what you want is to sell, your videos should also contain something more than advertising your business.

Think of your favorite TV commercials. What do these few-second-long commercials have that made you like them? Although companies make commercials just because they want to promote themselves or their products and services, they also include stories and interesting clips to their commercials to be able to attract viewers. The same thing also goes with YouTube videos.

For instance, if you want to create a one-minute YouTube video to promote your business, don't spend the entirety of that video just talking about your business. If you did so, chances are your viewers will leave your page as soon as they possibly can. So, think about the elements of your videos that will attract your audience and will create a good impression on them.

Start your video with something that will catch people's attention. It should be something that will make them feel like you're calling them to watch your video. Then continue with something that will boost their interests more. While you're into it, you can now insert your purpose to your new viewer.

Don't be too direct, though. Don't say things like "Buy this product!" or "Visit us at..." because that will just most likely push your viewers away. Instead, what you should do is to convince them to support your business through the things that you have shown on your videos.

HOW TO PRODUCE A GREAT
YOUTUBE VIDEO

Now that you have a foundation built on your brand, purpose, difference and target audience; the structural pieces in place with your website, blog and social media profiles; and have earned a following — it's time to start shooting your videos!

All the marketing, social media, blogging and promoting in the world won't earn you subscribers if your videos aren't interesting to watch. There's a lot of thought, planning and practice that went into my very first video. I've had over a decade of public speaking, presenting and marketing experience. Even if you don't have the experience I do, you too can be a success on YouTube.

Here are some practical tips for creating videos that will make your target audience fall in love with you and want to subscribe to your YouTube channel.

A. Subscribers Connect with People, Not RVs, Not Recipes, Not Music, Not Even Gorgeous Scenery

These things are your co-stars. YOU are the star. You need to make an appearance in every video — and no, your feet and hands don't count! In our increasingly anonymous, disconnected online society, people crave connection. And they need to see you to connect with you. Every video needs to have an up close and personal introduction, showing your face. A personal closing is also ideal — but not as mandatory as an intro. And if you can narrate throughout your scenic videos, even better. And include your four-legged family members as much as possible. People LOVE pets!!! Capone gets more fan mail than I do!

B. Tell Your Story

Who are you? Why are you doing what you're doing in life (whether its full time RVing or Vandwelling, cooking with 18th century technology or something else)? What motivates you? Why are you making videos? What's your message? Who are you trying to relay your message to? You may not address these questions directly when telling your story, but they must be part of the story, in some way. Your first video tells the world who you are, why you're doing what you're doing and why they should watch you.

Your story will be an integral part of every video you make. Know who you are and what your purpose is. Stay true to yourself and your mission and your audience will love you.

C. Be Authentic

There are a million and one bland, cookie-cutter, generic YouTube channels with a few hundred subscribers. These channels are hosted by people who are afraid that speaking their truth will rock the boat and they'll get criticized. Guess what? They're right! Guess what else? Playing it safe does not make a successful YouTube channel. I have been saying the same thing to business owners for years: you can't have success without risk!

Do you want to be free of criticism and risk or do you want to have a successful YouTube Channel? You can't have both!

The most successful YouTubers speak their truth; they aren't afraid to stir the pot and challenge people. Sure, you're going to get haters (trust me, I know), but you will either have to find a way to deal with that or forget about being a success on YouTube. AUTHENTICITY sells.

I'm not saying you should air your dirty laundry and drag your skeletons out of the closet to share with the world. What I AM saying is that whatever message or purpose you're compelled to deliver, do it authentically. If you find yourself holding back, white-washing, or diluting yourself or your message, chances are you're leaving opportunity on the table.

Be Interesting! Be funny, quirky, geeky, cute, irreverent, controversial or independent...but whatever you do, don't be boring!

D. What Is Your Channel's Theme?

What kind of channel are you creating? Will it be a how-to channel, with videos and advice for Do-it-Yourselfers? Will it be a travel Vlog? Will it be inspirational or spiritual in nature? Will you tell stories? Share cautionary tales? Share your philosophies on life? Or a combination of all of these?

Know this before you shoot your first video! Be clear about your intentions on your channel and follow through with that intention in each video; don't make the viewer guess what you, your channel, or any video is about. Title your channel and each video appropriately and tell your audience up front what you will cover in the video.

E. Prepare Your Talk!

If you aren't an experienced public speaker or presenter (or even if you are) preparation is your friend. Before you shoot a video, prepare an outline with the following:

1. The topic of the video.

2. What do you want people to gain/learn/understand/experience.

3. If it's a how-to or instructional video, create an outline of the points you want to cover. It's ok to refer to notes while you shot your video.

4. If it's a Vlog, what's your message or purpose? Yes, every video needs to have a purpose, even if you're just vlogging your day or a walk in the park! What do you hope your audience will walk away feeling, thinking or learning?

F. Practice! Practice! Practice!

Some of the feedback I get most on my YouTube channel is that people watch my videos, partly, because of how comfortable, inviting and warm I am in front of the camera. If you're camera shy, self-conscious, uncomfortable, unsure of yourself or your purpose or are unprepared, it will show. Humans pick up subconscious signals from others in nanoseconds, if you aren't at ease in front of the camera, your audience won't be at ease watching you. They may not even consciously be aware of their unease, but their subconscious will tell them something isn't right, and they'll click away. Possibly never to return.

When I began my sales career the company, I worked for sent me to a three-day class to learn how to create presentations and speak in public. They video-taped me more than ten times over three days and critiqued me, both one-on-one and in front of the group for three straight days. Yes, it was brutal, but I came away from that class a much better speaker and I honed my skills over the upcoming decade of public speaking and presenting.

If you're like me, you probably don't have $10,000 to spend on a course to teach you how to present and speak in front of a camera (neither did I, the company paid for it!). Don't fret! I am here to share with you the invaluable lessons I learned in that class and over 10+ years I've been presenting and speaking in front of large groups of business owners!

TIP: If you're stationary, look for a local ToastMasters group to join. ToastMasters is an international organization with local groups to help people become better public speakers. I've heard great things about the groups from colleagues who have become better speakers by joining.

Practical Video Shooting Tips

Choose a Great Setting for Your Videos! Your choice of setting will vary, depending on the theme of your YouTube channel. Whether you're an RV- or VanDweller, a Life-After-Divorce Coach or something else, choose an appropriate setting for your videos that reflects your Purpose and feeds your Target Audience the experience they're seeking.

Tips for making visually appealing videos:

1. Your Face. If the theme of your videos is YOU, then background and setting aren't as important as it is for others. All the audience wants to see is you. To pull this off, you need to be expressive, outgoing, fun and 100% real. YouTube stars who create channels about themselves are bold, brave and have strong personalities. If this is the type of channel you're creating, the camera will focus on your face.

2. LOCATON! LOCATION! LOCATION! If YOU aren't the theme of your channel, location matters. If you're a VanDweller or RVer like me — get out of your RV or Van! Seriously, that gets boring fast, unless YOU are the theme — but that's hard to pull off for most people. Make your 'set' visually appealing; go to a gorgeous location, take a few wardrobe options, and shoot multiple videos while you're there. Take a look at the most successful RV and VanDweller YouTubers, most of them shoot at fun and beautiful locations or show some other visually appealing content.

3. If you don't travel. If you don't travel and don't have awe inspiring vistas to use as your backdrop, create a warm an inviting space to shoot your videos. Make sure it's uncluttered, clean, warm and bright. Get out of your house, van or RV!!!

THE TOOLS YOU NEED

Video content is taking over the Internet. More and more people are preferring to consume information through videos on YouTube because they are more engaging, more urgent, and more entertaining. It becomes necessary to produce high-quality videos to attract more viewers and grow your subscriber base.

Set-Up

There are different ways to record a video for YouTube. The method would depend on the type of camera you have and the kind of video you intend to shoot. There are so many options when it comes to the type and brand of camera to use for recording videos. Instead of contemplating and worrying about camera brands, lens kit, and accessories, focus on the content and just use what you currently have. It could be an entry-level DLSR, a smartphone, a handheld camera, or a webcam. As long as it can record in high definition, it would do.

The important thing is to understand and master the basics of video recording. You only need to have a foundational knowledge of the camera and equipment to get started with video recording.

If you're just starting and don't want to spend a lot of money, you could buy the camera that's within your budget and just upgrade to a better camera that would satisfy your video recording needs.

Cameras

In choosing a camera, you must first decide what kind of video content you'll be doing. If you are doing mostly a talking-head video where you're just talking to the camera, you don't need a full-featured camera. What you intend to do with your videos will help you decide which camera to use.

Here are the types of cameras you can choose from:

•Point-and-shoot cameras

These no-fuss cameras are so easy to use that you can use straight out of the box. You can select one of the many presets available depending on the type of video you're recording. They deliver full HD image quality and are ideal for vlogging.

•DSLR cameras

This is the camera to use if you want high-quality images in full HD. While it has the most professional-looking results, here is a learning curve before you can operate the camera properly. You have to learn how to focus the lens and be familiar with the settings. DSLR cameras are typically used in shooting scenes with cinematic effects. Videos shot with DSLR look more professional and well-thought-out.

•Smartphone Cameras — Although phone cameras now deliver high-quality images, they don't quite match up with standalone cameras. Many YouTube creators use their smartphones when they are vlogging. They use the selfie mode to record themselves as they go through their daily activities.

•Webcam – These are tiny cameras that you can use if you're doing video game walkthroughs, demos, and screenshare.

•Action Cameras – These are small compact cameras used to record first-person point of view of events. They are best used in capturing fast movement because of their superb image stabilization system. They are ideal for recording extreme sports and underwater shots.

Microphones

Your videos must have clear sounds. Viewers may tolerate shaky camera shots, but they can't stand poor audio. That's why it's important to use a microphone when shooting a video.

Cameras have their onboard microphone, but you would have to stay within three to four feet from the camera to capture the voice and sound. This setup wouldn't work if the subject you're filming has to be talking from a distance. An external microphone will help boost the audio quality.

Types of microphones

•Shotgun – This microphone has directional recording so they are effective in picking up sounds when pointed directly at the source of the sound.

•Lavalier – This microphone can be clipped onto your clothing (also called lapel mic). It's best used for interviews or when the subject is far from the camera.

•Boom — This microphone is used to capture dialogues or conversations among several people. It's connected to a long pole so that it can be held above the frame of the scene. This is used in film-making because it can capture natural sounds effectively.

Lighting

Lighting is important in creating high-quality videos. This is something that many creators take for granted. Lighting is more than just making sure viewers see your subject, it also creates the tone and mood of the video.

Different kinds of lighting setups and techniques can influence how your video would be perceived by the viewers. If you want your viewers to feel a certain way when they watch your videos, lighting can help give tonal cues that will match the message that you're trying to convey.

Lighting can also be used to guide your viewers where to look. It can naturally draw their eyes on the specific part of the video you want them to focus on. High contrast images can make objects in your videos stand out. Although you can make adjustments in post-production, it will save you a great deal of time and grief if you start with proper lighting. With great lighting, your videos will look professional and pleasing to the eyes.

Here are the most common lighting setups that can make your videos a whole lot better.

•Two-point lighting system. This uses two light sources at opposite ends. The first light source is the "key light" which provides the primary lighting to the subject. The second light called "fill light" balances out the shadows.

•Three-point lighting system. In addition to the key light and the fill light, this setup uses a backlight that splits the subject and the background.

•Natural light. There's nothing better than natural light coming from the sun. You can record outdoors at certain times of the day when the light is at its brightest. Alternatively, you can record near a window so you can take advantage of natural light coming in. The downside to this is that it's a little trickier to control, but it can be done.

Accessories

•Tripod – Unless you really intend to make shaky action videos, you must use a tripod to stabilize your shots.

•Teleprompter – A video teleprompter is not required but it can help you create more content faster. You can structure your content so that you don't waste time going off-topic. Since you're reading from a teleprompter, you can minimize mistakes. The fewer mistakes you make, the faster the editing can be done.

Best Tools with YouTube:

Plenty of useful tools exists to use with YouTube, including video creation tools, video promotion tools, and more. Making use of these will help you grow your subscribers in an organic way, and organic views mean more subscribers, over time. Here are some video marketing tools you can use to get the results you're looking for.

• Bulk Suggest Tool: This free tool was created by the Internet Marketing Ninjas and is an easy way to find out relevant keyword research data for your content. It will look through YouTube and Google's "auto complete" databases, expanding the terms you entered based on popular search terms. This allows you to compare search terms in Google fast with YouTube terms, better understanding the searching goals of your target subscribers and audience members.

• WordPress Keyword Plugin: In addition, there's a plugin for WordPress that you can use to look at keyword ideas using Google auto complete search terms. This is in your dashboard under the post editing options. Another benefit to this plugin is that it can give ideas for what to create articles and videos about based on what is popular.

HOW TO WRITE A GREAT TITLE
AND DESCRIPTION

Writing Great Title

Your title is your chance to make a good first impression. This is the first thing people see before they decide which videos to click. Based on the title, they will decide if your video is worth their time. If they find that your title matches exactly what they are looking for, then your video will surely get a click.

There's no magic formula that guarantees a click-worthy title, but there are ways to make your titles stand out.

- Use 10 words or less. It should be short and to the point.
- Include numbers if you are making a video listicle (e.g. 8 Strategies To Get More YouTube Subscribers)
- Include the specific benefit of your video.
- Add the keyword or phrase in the title.

When it comes to YouTube videos, your titles are everything. The title is one of the first things a viewer sees and often determines whether or not he or she will watch that video. For the best results, you should put some extra effort in to make sure that the titles of your video are appealing and inviting. Let's take a look at some keys for writing a good title:

Write descriptive titles. For example, if you uploaded a video of your dog doing tricks, avoid titles such as my dog or beagle playing. Titles like those don't tell you much about what's going on in the video. A better example of a good title would be Beagle Performs Amazing Tricks Video. From this title, you know that the video will be of a beagle dog doing something that you may not see every day.

Include the word video in your title. Many people search for videos in Google instead of directly in YouTube, so a typical search would be something like dog trick video and yours would likely turn up in the search results.

As always, be sure to do extensive keyword research for your title to make sure that you're using the best combination of words.

In addition to having a great thumbnail image and several keywords, you also need to have a captivating title and a good description. Your title is going to help entice people to click on your video and watch it. It will work hand in hand with your thumbnail image to capture interest and spark curiosity. Therefore, make sure you have a captivating title that will tell viewers exactly what they are going to watch. People like to know what is coming in the future. They don't want to be surprised and they definitely don't want to be disappointed.

When writing your title try to write it in keyword segments. However, unlike in the tag, you are going to spell thing properly and make it look nice. Your title is something that needs to be appealing. Remember, people judge books by the cover so if the title looks bad then they are going to pass right on to the other one. The same is true with your video. People are going to decide based on your thumbnail and then your title whether or not they want to watch your video. Although on YouTube you will always have a thumbnail, in some search engines your thumbnail will not display. That means it is up to your title to draw them in. Therefore, make sure it is nice.

Your title and thumbnail must work together to draw people to your video.

Therefore, write your title in two or three different search phrases that tell exactly what the video is about. It is a good idea to use dividers between the phrases so that people can easily read them without having to strain their eyes. Things like dashes – or vertical bars | will work nicely. In addition, try to place your brand at the end of your title so that people will know your videos even when the thumbnail isn't present. This is mostly for off YouTube promotion like when your title is hyperlinked on another site or on social media.

Writing Great Descriptions

It's vital to place a description on your videos so as to assist people find your own videos. But just allow it to be certain that you leverage key words and hashtags. Your movie's name and description need to have the content which informs people what is going to expect to see if they will see your movie. Adding a backlink to your site from the description is also a wise idea to get off people to YouTube and on your site.

Just like your channel description, your video description must be optimized as well. YouTube will factor in the description in the ranking algorithm. If you write your description with search engine optimization in mind, your video will have a better chance of being discovered.

Follow these simple rules of thumb:

- Should be at least 150 words.
- Include the target keywords
- Focus on the first two sentences. Only the first two sentences

will appear below your video; the rest of the description will only appear when viewers click on "Show More".

- Include your call-to-action pitch. If you are asking people to sign up or join something, you have to provide the link to the website.
- Include the affiliate links if you're doing product reviews.
- Include links to your website and social media.
- Don't use misleading or clickbaity titles. Misrepresenting the content of our video will turn your viewers away and avoid your videos like a plague.
- Deliver what you promise.

HOW TO UPLOAD AND EDIT A
VIDEO TO YOUTUBE

Uploading Your Videos

After putting the finishing touches on your video, it's finally time to upload your hard work. Open up YouTube and access your account. On the top-right side of your web page, you'll see an "Upload" button which will take you to an upload landing page. On it, you'll see a large "Drag and Drop" button to upload your files directly onto the browser. Once you've dragged the file and dropped it to initiate the upload (which takes a while, depending on the size of your video and the speed of your internet connection), you'll be directed to a video details page where you can input the video's name and Meta tags. Spend some time figuring out the tags since that will play a crucial part in the ease with which people find your content through the YouTube search engine—claimed by some to be the second largest search engine in the world.

The easiest way to figure out popular tags is to break down your content into its basic elements—if you're making a tutorial video, add "How-To", "Tutorial", "DIY", or whichever other tag would be appropriate. Be sure to not over-crowd the bar, and cram in as many tags as you can think of. Most people don't realize it, but today's search engines automatically place such content with an overwhelming number of tags lower among search results. Also, some monetization options such as Google AdSense have strict policies against supporting video content with too many tags. You can also simply enter the text which you think your potential viewers would ask into the search engine to see which other tags you could enter. Don't make tags overly specific as that will narrow down the scope of the audience which could potentially be led to your doorstep. Think about it—if you opened a restaurant, even if it were an unusual Nordic-Thai fusion food place, you wouldn't put up signs saying "Come right along, for people who want to experience the ultimate clash between two cultures who never rightly met in medieval times. Perfect for those times of weird craving you never knew you had, when you wish you could get some Lutefisk served on a bed of Pad Thai". No, you'd say, "Yum Yum. Awesome Grub. Step right here", or something of the sort— you get my point.

Once you've finished uploading the video and added the Meta tags, click the social media icons and add a personalized message which would send a note to all your subscribers while informing them of the new upload on your channel—once you get subscribers, that is, but don't ever let that hold you back from marketing your content on social media especially since these platforms provide the quickest way to rapidly increasing the exposure of your intellectual offerings.

Finally, once the video has finished uploading, you will receive the option of three thumbnails from which you can select one to serve as your video's thumbnail while viewing it within a list as a visitor. Although this option may not be immediately available as soon as you upload your first video, you will also receive the option of uploading and using a custom thumbnail instead from your computer. This may serve you better if you don't like any of the choices among the auto-generated thumbnails provided by YouTube.

While we aren't discussing monetization options yet, once you do have them enabled—you will be able to activate monetization of your videos from within these settings themselves.

Furthermore, another impressive feature available in YouTube is the "Creator Studio"—available as an option once you click on your picture icon on the top right side of the YouTube page. Once you access that feature, you'll be taken to your channel dashboard, where all the relevant analytics of your work will be available, with your total number of subscribers, total views, and the estimated minutes of your content watched by viewers. It would be a great way to check whether most viewers watch the entirety of your content or tune out after a point.

This is also the feature which you'll have to access if you wish to upload videos longer than 15-minutes. Click on the "Channel" option visible on the left-hand side column in the Creator Studio page, and search for the "Longer Videos" tab under "Feature".

On the left-hand side, you'll see a column with the option of "Video Manager" available therein. Upon accessing this option, you'll be taken to a list of your published content, with options to publish, remove, or monetize videos with the click of a button (after you've enabled Monetization methods).

Editing Your Videos

Watch time, retention rate, and clickthrough rate are YouTube's three most important metrics. We'll talk about clickthrough rate, but the watch time and retention rate are both critical parts of the creation process.

The best way to thrive with these two metrics other than creating quality content is through quality editing. Video editing can turn a good video into a great one with multiple angles, audio effects, and other pattern interrupts.

There are plenty of tools available to edit your videos. Free ones like iMovie and Movie Maker give plenty of options. While Adobe

Premiere Pro is a popular choice among YouTubers who have been at it for a while, I personally prefer to use ScreenFlow to edit my videos.

A general rule of thumb for editing videos is to have at least one pattern interrupt every minute. Anything from an audio effect to a different camera angle qualifies. Incorporating more of these pattern interrupts will make your videos more engaging.

If you prefer to delegate the video editing, I recommend finding someone on onlinejobs.ph, Fiverr, or UpWork to get the job done. You'll either have to pay video editors on a per video or per hour basis. If you produce many videos that require minimal editing, the per hour basis would be the better approach. If you want highly detailed editing for each of your videos, you should find a video editor who will charge you per video instead of per hour.

In either case, your video script will play a key role in speeding up your video editor's time. The video script doesn't just contain everything you want to say. It also contains all of the video edits you want to see in the video and when you want to see them. This will make it easier for you or the person you hire depending on which approach you take.

Without a video script like the one above, video editing can be extremely tedious. Video editing can still take a considerable amount of time even with the script, but you'll easily save at least 30 minutes with the script in place.

YOUTUBE SEO

We will show you exactly how you can best optimize your videos for highest search rankings. You'll learn all the steps you need to take from uploading your videos, to publishing and boosting your video. You'll also learn all the YouTube ranking factors that affect your rankings.

Important: Combining both On-Page and Off-Page SEO methods is a surefire way to get the best ranking results. Remember to always test, test, test, and track what you do so you can see what is or isn't working and repeat the steps at a future date.

Upload Your Videos

After editing your video, it's time to upload it to YouTube. But before you upload it, there are a few things you must do to optimize it.

1) Prepare Your Video

YouTube and Google both look at the filenames and file meta data to check for context and keywords. Therefore, to optimize ranking ability, you'll need to get it ready before you upload.

2) Filenames and Meta

What you need to do is set the name of the video and thumbnail image file the keyword phrase. This will give YouTube a clearer idea about what your video is about.

Then, depending on the operating system you're using, you can edit the video file properties and add meta tags. I add the main keyword in there as well, both for the video and the thumbnail.

3) Upload as Private

Tip: I highly recommend uploading your video as private so you can add all your video details and get everything ready to go before you publish it. Once you publish it, you have a limited window of time where YouTube will gauge the number of views and interaction within the first few hours to 24 hours.

YouTube Video Ranking Factors

You'll learn about all the different factors that affect your video ranking and the ones that YouTube looks for when it is determining how high it should rank your video for a certain keyword.

I want to credit Stoica for a similar diagram he shared with me in one of his newsletter emails about all the different factors that YouTube looks for when ranking a video.

I've adapted and re-created the diagram for a more modern look, and you can also view it online, share it on social media, or even embed it on your blog or website.

You can download the full diagram here: vidtr.in/factors

Title, Tags, Description – These are the "on-page" SEO factors, or the text that goes with the video that gives context and allows YouTube to determine what the video is about. Along with this is the video filename, captions (aka closed captions or cc), annotations, outgoing links, and content uniqueness (text that is unique and not copy-pasted from elsewhere).

Number of Views – YouTube looks at the number of views on both your video, your channel, and overall views across all of your videos. It also takes into account the source of the views, how many initial views the video gets within the first 24-48 hours, and very importantly, the view retention. View retention means how long out of the total length of the video does the viewer watch. There are two types of view retention: relative retention and absolute retention.

Relative retention is when YouTube compares the retention rate to similar length videos. Absolute retention is how long you keep your viewers engaged on your specific video and whether there any points in the video that keep them engaged longer than normal.

Keywords – This factor includes the length of the description, using the exact match of the keyword phrase, the keyword in the title, description and tags, and also having some secondary similar keywords sprinkled in there.

Channel – The channel name, number of subscribers, total number of videos, age of the channel, and the SEO in the channel description and tags all play a role in how well your video ranks.

Backlinks – These are links from other sites that point toward your video or channel. Important elements include the anchor text (text of the link), the number of backlinks, and the quality of the backlinks (Trust Flow, Domain Authority), and number of videos embeds.

Sharing – Social signals are very important and gives an indication how interesting and engaging a video is. This includes shares on various social media platforms, especially Google+, Facebook, Blogger, LinkedIn and Twitter. Likes, favorites, pluses and retweets are all counted toward this factor.

Interaction – YouTube wants its users to stay on its platform and engage with the content and community. Therefore, interaction plays a huge part in gauging how relevant a video is. Elements like how many playlists a video is added to, the number of comments on the video, if any relevant keywords are in the comments, and the number of likes and dislikes.

On-Page Video SEO

On-page SEO refers to every element you need to optimize that has to do with the video and the video page itself.

1) Video Filename

Before you upload your video you YouTube, you want to make sure the video filename has your main keyword in it. Do this with the video thumbnail as well. If possible, I also add the main keyword in the meta tags of the file. Depending on your operating system, you can do this by editing the file properties.

2) Video Title

The video title is the most important on-page SEO element of your video. You'll need to include the main keyword in here, as close as you can to the front. Then I recommend including a secondary YouTube keyword as well, separated by a pipe | symbol or hyphen.

For example, if your keyword is "how to make money on YouTube" and your secondary keyword is "how I make money on YouTube fast", then it would look like:

How To Make Money On YouTube – How I Make Money On YouTube Fast!

Tip: In addition to adding your keyword, it helps to craft an attention-grabbing headline around it for maximum attention-grabbing potential.

For example, I could transform the above into:

How To Make Money On YouTube – Watch How I Make Money on YouTube Fast in 24 Hours | With PROOF!

Now it reads more powerful and makes searchers want to click on the headline.

Alternatively, if you just want to go for a viral headline, go to BuzzSumo.com and enter your keyword. Look at the top trending article headlines for this topic and model one of them. If possible, try to include your keyword in the headline you write, otherwise you wouldn't be optimizing your video for ranking.

3) Video Tags

The video tags are a very important element that helps YouTube and Google understand what your video is about. This is how to create your tags:

Let's say the keyword is again, "how to make money on YouTube". I would create my tags like this:

How to make money on YouTube, how to make money, make money on YouTube, how to, make money, YouTube

In other words, I would include my main keyword, then chunk it down smaller and smaller.

Then, I would go on YouTube and search my main keyword. I would then click on the first ranked video and grab the tags in that video.

Super Tip: Now, here's a ninja secret not many people know – normally, YouTube hides tags from the public, BUT if you're using Google Chrome Browser, or a browser that allows you to view the html, you can right click on the page and then select "view source". Then type ctrl+f (PC) or cmd+f (Mac), and type in "tags". There should be a list of tags that you can copy and paste at the end of your own list.

Why are we doing this? Because for this keyword, YouTube has determined it is the most relevant, so by mirroring the tags, YouTube will see your video as closely related and will rank it higher in the search results.

4) Video Description

The description is also a very important element that cannot be underestimated. The first three lines are the most important for two reasons: firstly, because it's the only part that's visible by default, until you click on the link to expand it. Secondly, because YouTube values the first lines the most in terms of looking for relevant keywords and understanding the meaning.

Tip: What you need to do is put your main keyword in the first line, as close as you can to the front. If possible, copy and paste your title in the first line instead of including something else. The first three lines is also where you would put your main call to action link that you want people to visit.

For the rest of the description, you'll need at least 300 words of content relating to the video keyword. Ideally, it would be 800-1,000 words so YouTube has more context to work with, but 300 is fine. You can either write the content or paste the transcript in there.

Important: Make sure the main keyword is in there at least once somewhere in the middle, and at least once near the end. Sprinkle some related keywords and some of the tags in there as well, but do it naturally, you don't want to "keyword stuff", which could have negative consequences.

Add a few links into your description back to YouTube to give yourself some backlinks. Include a link back to the same video, and a link to your channel, and also a link to a video that is ranking in the top 3 positions for your keyword.

You should also link out to an authority blog post about that topic that gives YouTube and Google some more context to work with to understand your video better.

Closed Captions

By default, YouTube uses machine transcription to turn any speech into text for the closed captions or subtitles. Naturally, it's not perfect and can make errors, so it's best to edit and fix them.

Alternatively, you can get your video professionally transcribed and then upload the new subtitles and set them as default.

Transcribe Your Video

The slow and painful (but free) way to transcribe your audio would be to do it yourself, however it's not fun, and can take up a lot of time you could use to focus on more content instead.

Tools & Resources: I would recommend using a really good service called Rev.com where you can get videos transcribed and turned into closed captions for only $1 a minute.

If you want to reach a larger audience, you can also get your closed captions translated into another language, but it's not necessary.

5) Publish Your Video

Once you have your video details entered and your thumbnail uploaded, you're ready to publish it. As soon as you do, start sharing it on social media, and start building backlinks and embeds. This is when off-page video SEO comes into play.

Off-Page Video SEO

Off-page video SEO has to do with every element that needs to be optimized off the main video or channel page, like links pointing to the video or channel from other YouTube videos/channels, or external websites or social media profiles. Social mentions and activity also play a large role in off-page SEO.

Backlinks

What is a backlink? A backlink is simply a link that is pointing from another website, video, or social media profile to your page.

Why are backlinks important?

Think of each backlink as a vote, and each vote has different levels of authority. Just in the same way that 100 testimonials from people you don't know will have less influence than 10 testimonials from celebrities or industry leaders.

The more votes a website has, and the higher the authority, the more the website is likely to be trustworthy and relevant in the eyes of

Google or YouTube. This means it's more likely to rank higher for any given relevant search term.

Why do I need high quality backlinks?

When we talk about "high quality" backlinks, I'm mainly referring to the domain authority (DA) and page authority (PA) score. The higher the domain or page authority, the more ranking "power" it has.

Tools & Resources: Moz.com "Open Site Explorer" tool allows you to check pages' Domain Authority and Page Authority.

What's also really important is relevant backlinks. Let's say your video is about "how to train your parrot to talk", then you'll want backlinks from websites, blogs, forums, and other videos and channels that closely relate to the topic. Otherwise, the links would count much less or even change the context of your video topic.

How do you get high quality backlinks?

There are two ways you can do it: Do it yourself or outsource them. Both have their pros and cons.

Building your own backlinks can be a lot of work and takes time, but you have more control over it and have full transparency of where you link from. It can also be less expensive if done through guest posts, on your own websites, or other free ways.

Outsourcing backlinks can be a tricky minefield if you don't know what to look for. The advantage is you save a lot of time.

There are a lot of sellers on the market where their backlinks just don't work or could even harm your video ranking performance. On the other hand, if you find the right providers, you'll be able to scale up your efforts without extra time.

A good place to look for backlinks is Fiverr.com or SEOClerks.com. The best way to determine whether the backlinks are good are to purchase from top rated sellers with a lot of 5-star reviews, and finally, just test and track your results using a keyword rank tracking software. If they are quality backlinks, your video should start seeing some ranking improvements.

Tools & Resources:

SEO Clerks - vidtr.in/seoclerks

This is an amazing platform for all services relating to SEO, from buying backlinks, social signals, and much more. Make sure you buy from a trusted provider by looking at the ratings first.

You may have to test many providers before you find ones that work best. Always make sure they do "whitehat" and Google-friendly practices, so your video or channel won't get penalized for bad links.

Video Embedding

Embedding your video on external websites is also a signal that YouTube looks for when ranking your video. You should embed your videos on your website and blogs to get more backlinks and external views on your videos, all which contribute to helping your ranking.

Again, make sure you embed on relevant pages and websites that relate to your video topic.

Video Playlists

Add your video into a relevant playlist. Playlists are searchable in YouTube, so create a playlist with relevant videos, including your own, and use a similar keyword. This will definitely boost your ranking, even if just a little bit.

Social Signals

Social media has become increasingly important, not only as a way to connect & engage with your audience, but also for search engines to determine how popular and relevant a website or video is by looking at social signals.

What are social signals?

Social signals are any activity on social media platforms that mention or link to your video or channel page. They include engagement signals like shares, likes, favorites, and comments.

Build backlinks to your video by posting it on social media. You will also be able to reach a lot more people and get people to watch and interact with your video. If they share it, you'll get the added benefit of reaching an even larger network you wouldn't have been able to otherwise.

Action Step: Post your video on as many as your social media platform as possible, like Google+, Facebook, Twitter, LinkedIn, Pinterest, Instagram and others.

Why are social signals important?

YouTube or Google are smart, but they can't evaluate whether the video content itself is actually any good. They rely on social signals and the reactions of others to see how interesting a video is.

The idea is, the more shares, likes, and comments a post has, the more engaging and interesting a video is assumed to be.

How to get more social engagements on your videos

If you want to get more social interaction and engagements on your video posts in social media, try these ideas:

- •Have an eye-catching thumbnail that stops the viewer from scrolling down the feed
- •Add a benefit-based, curiosity-instilling headline
- •Let them know what's in it for them, what will they learn?
- •Tell them exactly what to do: LIKE, COMMENT, and SHARE!
- •Post at times when most of your audience is active on the platform (use TubeBuddy.com)

Tools & Resources:

TubeBuddy - vidtr.in/tbud

This Google Chrome plugin is also a must-have for any YouTuber. It has way more features than VidIQ and adds advanced functionality to YouTube such as bulk processing, video SEO, promotion, and data research. There are too many features to mention here, but in short, it makes things so much easier and faster to use. Definitely download and install it.

HOW TO CREATE VIDEOS THAT CONVERT

Before jumping on the bandwagon and producing videos to upload on YouTube, it is important to know what contents attract traffic and how they are presented. Cat videos are awesome but earning three figures from it is also a long shot. At the same time, overcomplicated productions may only cost more than what it is actually worth.

As mentioned before, higher views mean higher passive income; therefore, the video needs to attract a wider demographic. To achieve this, its information and entertainment value needs to be carefully measured and balanced.

To make brainstorming less strenuous, you can use the following as reference. This will also serve as the initial step in creating videos for passive income.

Tutorial Videos

Also known as how-to videos, these are basically among the easiest to produce. Everyone is an expert of something, and experience and knowledge are the only requirements for it. This can be a tutorial of any skill. Some of the most popular videos are demonstrations of:

- The use of software and programs
- Craft-making and various constructions
- Repairs
- Hobbies (i.e. playing an instrument, gardening, and such)
- Sharing self-developed techniques and secrets can assure high views. In fact, these are what people look for in tutorials.

Notes:

- Determine if the demonstration is for beginners, intermediates, or experts. This can affect the scope of interested viewers, and thus the amount of passive income. Understand that introductory tutorials always have a wider audience, because the video addresses the problem of everyone who doesn't have the know-how in the most basic level. In contrast, expert level how-to's will always be limited to the number of people who already have advanced knowledge on the skill.
- Fewer minutes are always more appreciated in how-to videos. People look for straightforward and concise answers to their problems. Spending time on answering unimportant questions like who, when, where and why will only drive the audience away.

Explanation Videos or Documentaries

Think NatGeo, History Channel and Discovery when considering this type of video. It's not the cinematography that matters, however, but the questions being answered. Apart from the how, it should explain the what, when, where, who and why. The information presented should also be backed up by studies and statistics for increased viability.

These videos aren't limited to dragging subjects as well. There are

YouTuber geniuses who regularly come up with simple but attention-catching topics. They focus on answering or explaining little facts, like why Americans are circumcised, or where the best vintage cars are located. Darker subjects also continue to captivate the curiosity of audience, like Illuminati secrets and alien conspiracies.

Notes:

- First of all, adequate knowledge and background on a chosen topic is needed. Being careless in presenting information can only lead to a damaged reputation.
- Ideal video length is fifteen to twenty minutes for simple and fun topics, whereas more serious ones may require hours. This video is given bigger time allowances because every question has to be answered. Its objective is to leave the audience with solid information on the subject and should never be left with more questions.

Interactive Videos

YouTube's developers enabled uploaders to place annotations or captions where links can be inserted; therefore, if a video needs to be linked to a website or another video, the URL, or a button containing the link, can flash or appear as the audience watch. Despite the existence of other video sites, this is only doable in YouTube.

With a touch of creativity, some YouTubers managed to produce quizzes. For example, a single video upload will hold a question, and end with multiple choice answers. Audiences can click on an answer, which will then take them to another video that opens either a second question if the answer is correct, or a clickable try again note to restart the game.

Apart from quizzes, making story consequence games is also possible. Videos will present a story, then at the end, viewers can select what ending they want it to have. This can lead to another upload showing the conclusion, or one that opens another sequence of events and set of possible endings.

The interaction initiated by these videos will spark and maintain interest and whenever it's worth spending time with, it's also worth sharing with friends. Despite greater efforts in producing one, the possibility of getting a hundred thousand views isn't farfetched.

NOTES:

•Interactive videos can be in any length. As long as its entertainment value exceeds expectations, it can be longer, or in this case, more complicated.

•Creativity will always define a video from the rest; therefore, even if the link to be placed is for only a simple website, it is still advisable to make an effort to create a button for it.

VLOGS

Otherwise known as video blogs, the contents of these can basically be about anything and everything. Furthermore, not much research is needed because personal opinions will weigh more. These can be:

•Reviews for movies, books, games, and products

•Personal perspective on budding issues

•Travel experiences

•Random blurb

•Basically, whatever can be written down in blog can be said in a vlog. There's no need for complicated productions. People can literally just place a webcam before themselves then talk. Despite the simplicity, vlogs are very popular, and views can reach up to millions.

NOTES:

•The more sensational the topic is, the more it will attract viewers - the legalization of same sex marriage, for example. Downside of this, however, is that it's prone to receiving negative comments from other users. But then again, the more negativity, the more likely it is to become viral.

•Aiming for a wider audience means steering away from niched subjects. Topics should be something everybody can relate to. This is why reactions on politics, entertainment industry, and blockbuster movies are always opted for.

•The shorter the video, the better. Just like in blogs, people prefer reading fewer blocks of text. The same is expected in vlogs. Once the main point has been stated, it's time to conclude the video.

Participation or Let's Play Videos

This is similar with a vlog, only that opinions are narrated over something. For example, gamers could record their game, then as they play, they speak out their commentary. Apart from production differences, what sets participation videos from vlogs is how it doesn't always have to focus on opinions. In fact, what the audience look for in this are reactions.

Some of the most popular participation videos are horror games where the players' faces are recorded.

•Again, something that everyone can relate to is preferable and though this is more popular among games, this video is also applicable on MV's or sensitive movies and books (i.e. Fifty Shades of Grey). One of the fast-rising channels today is Fine Brothers Entertainment. They presented interesting settings like kids react to old computers, or teens react to 90's internet, and the reaction they get from guests are something between noteworthy, adorable and funny.

•These are often given longer times, depending on what would be reacted on. Some games, for example, last for hours, and the audience will watch it from start to finish. Creative uploaders, on the other hand, cut the video to pieces and only combine scenes with relevant reactions or narration.

Stunts, Dares and Pranks

As the name suggests, the focus of these videos is on entertainment. There's no need for it to be instilled with information because people will solely watch it for amusement.

Stunts can range from skateboard tricks and cycling dares, to cliff jumps and skydives. What will bring views in are 1) impressive and unique techniques, or 2) breathtaking and dangerous environments.

As for pranks, crazier is better. This, however, will also mean more complications in the production. Playing tricks on roommates is good but taking it in public will definitely bring the house down.

Perhaps, the easiest to produce among the three are dares. These can be as simple as eating a spoonful of cinnamon or dressing up like Nicki Minaj and walking in public.

NOTE:

•These videos have the least limitations. It can last for mere seconds or extend to twenty minutes, and people will love them all the same. As long as awesomeness is in every frame, it would make it impossible for the audience to click close.

•These are more suitable for travelers and stunt devils. Forcing oneself to perform something he's not capable of doing could only result to injuries; therefore, if going places and doing things are a regular thing, investing on a GoPro wouldn't be a bad idea. It could even bridge passion and passive income

•The limitation should be in the type of stunt, dare or prank to perform. These are not far from injuries and doing it for the sake of uploading a video on YouTube is never worth the possible damage.

Few of the videos enumerated above will require great effort in recording and editing. That's why when choosing a type of video, always consider your own availability, money and ability.

Increase Conversions

The main idea behind any form of marketing is knowing that you are making conversions. What does this mean? To a business owner, it means that they are converting their views into sales leads. An interesting thing about YouTube marketing is that you might have thousands of viewers with limited conversion rate. This means that you will not be benefiting from your marketing efforts. In fact, chances are that you might end up giving up since there are no fruits for you to enjoy.

Besides yearning to get more viewers on your YouTube business channel, you also need to make sure that you are getting something out of it. You need to find out whether you are getting more sales leads from your marketing or not. This can be evaluated, e.g. through gauging the amount of traffic that comes from your channel. If many people that are accessing your business page are from YouTube, then it means that your marketing efforts are up to par.

In the world of video marketing, there is a lot that you need to consider besides the fact that you are looking for a huge viewership. You need people to be impressed with your content to the point where they convert into customers. After that, you also need to work to convert the few customers you have into loyal clients.

So, how do you increase your conversion rate from the YouTube videos that you post?

Employ Other Click Strategy

After your audiences have watched the video, what else do you want from them? This is something that should ring in your mind as you create your YouTube videos. The idea here is that you need to motivate your followers to do something desirable after watching your video. In this case, it could be that you want them to visit your business website. Thus, you should provide them with directives that will help them in visiting your business website.

Say you are promoting the online education services that you are offering. Here, the best strategy would be to remind your audience on how to start the course. Therefore, there should be a button where they can click and begin the course. This link should direct them to your business page. Your videos need to be efficient in guaranteeing that you get the most out of the few seconds or minutes that your audiences are listening. So, don't waste time; get to the point.

Use an Attractive Thumbnail

When you are out shopping for a can of soda, there are times when you might get confused since there are many sodas to choose from. However, you end up picking one that has attractive packaging. Well, this is how thumbnails will help you stand out in the world of YouTube. When a user does their search, they are given several search results to choose from. So, what makes your brand different? Is it appealing from the first glimpse? Does it appeal to your audience better as compared to other video posts?

Using an attractive thumbnail comes highly recommended. It is what gives your brand an identity among other brands. Accordingly, if you design a good thumbnail, you can be sure that you will pull several people to watch your videos. From there, the quality of your video content will determine whether you will lure customers to depend on your products or not.

Motivate Viewers to Subscribe

Your conversion rate will also be greatly improved if you have many subscribers. The number of subscribers will indicate whether your content is performing well or not. A low subscriber rate signifies that your content is not alluring to your audience and they don't find any reason to raise their interest in the products or services that you offer. This could happen because you are selling to the wrong people and you will get several dislikes on your videos.

You need to motivate your viewers to subscribe to your business channel. Give them something to look forward to by offering them informative content that they cannot miss out on. The best part is that YouTube will reward you if you manage to get many people subscribing to your channel. Therefore, this means more money for your business. What's more, many subscribers on your channel also imply that your brand will have authority as compared to rival brands.

Work to Ensure Videos Are Watched to the End

The length of time that your viewers spend watching your videos will tell a lot about your content. If your viewers watch your videos to the end, it means that they were interested. They wanted to find out more about your company and the products or services that you offer. On the contrary, videos that are not watched to the end could mean that they are not entertaining. Maybe your introduction was not catchy enough. Make sure that your videos are watched to the end.

Evaluating the length of time your viewers watch your videos can be done by using the Watch Time metric. It tells you the amount of time spent on your video. As a result, you get to improve where you think that your videos are not performing well.

Playlists

Nothing beats the convenience that one finds when listening to their favorite music on YouTube. If there is a specific artist with songs that you love, YouTube makes your life easy by giving you a full playlist of their songs. Your playlist will, therefore, continue playing until you choose other songs.

The point here is that your brand should also have a playlist of its own. Your audience should not be lured to depend on other brands when you can offer them what they are looking for. Thus, you need to invest in your playlist to warrant that the eyeballs are only glued to your brand and nothing else.

Partner with Non-Competitive Channels

You could transform your sales overnight if at all you partner with the right YouTube personalities. Manufacturers understand how this works. There are those manufacturers that have teamed up with popular YouTube personalities to market their products for free. This means that they offer their products to be used freely by YouTube marketers. In the end, it is a win-win situation for them. They get more customers coming their way.

Equally, you could also leverage the benefits of partnering with brands that you are not competing with. For instance, if you are dealing with complementary products, you could work together to strengthen your authority on YouTube.

With these few pointers, you can increase your conversion rate on YouTube. The main thing is to focus on the customer. Understand what they need first. Thereafter, conduct research on ideal ways of meeting their needs. A satisfied customer will always tell their story to their friends on social media. The power of social media should help you in marketing your product without having to spend a lot. What your followers need is information that is pleasing to them. If you find a way of melting their hearts, you will find YouTube marketing as exciting. Your competitors will always wonder how you market your brand so easily. The trick is that it all depends on the message that you craft to your audience. So, play your cards right.

YOUTUBE MONETIZATION

For some YouTubers, creating a successful YouTube channel is an exercise in popularity. Their main intent is to become famous and achieve celebrity status.

For others, a successful YouTube channel is all about the opportunity to monetize it.

In short, monetization refers to the act of producing an income from a YouTube channel.

Some of the most successful YouTubers have become millionaires in the blink of an eye. Many of these new Internet celebrities are just ordinary folks who found a niche and made it their own. In time, these celebrities are flooded with endorsement offers in addition to advertiser dollars finding their way into their accounts.

The true metric of success on YouTube is the number of subscribers a channel has. The most successful channels have tens of millions of subscribers. Even if the majority of those subscribers are not diehard fans, they are, nonetheless, exposed to their contents. Besides, this is what advertisers crave.

Brands whose core customers live in the digital world may find YouTube as an excellent means of engaging them. This engagement can be augmented by piggybacking on those successful channels which have proven to draw a brand's target audience.

Indeed, those channels which are able to monetize their content might not only be able to make a decent income but might even catapult individual YouTubers into millionaire status.

That being said, a channel does not need to have 35 million subscribers in order to become monetized. Also, a regular brand and channel may be able to generate significant income for its owners.

This is the reason why YouTube has become so popular among average individuals. It's not only free but it is also a means of making money. When done right, YouTube can become a gold mine and a great way to earn a living without actually having to hold down a full-time job.

Whatever the purpose for creating a channel, YouTube offers a little bit of everything for everyone.

So, let's have a look at the different ways in which videos and channels may be monetized.

Tip #1: Build your AdSense strategy

Whoever said that there's no such thing as a free lunch was spot on. While YouTube may not charge a fee to users for access to its platform, it does find a way to make money from viewers.

Thus, YouTube will attach ads to any kind of content that gains traction. Of course, channels and videos with little to no viewers will get passed up, but those that gain some popularity will show up on the YouTube algorithm's radar.

This is where having an AdSense strategy pays off.

In short, AdSense means that your channel has been deemed

successful enough in order to make payments based on advertising linked to your channel.

When this occurs, your channel is ready to be monetized. Your channel will receive a cut from all of the viewer interaction with advertising linked to your channel. So, the more engagement you have with viewers, the more earning potential your channel has.

AdSense has rather strict guidelines and policies which must be followed. However, basically, eligible content needs to be devoid of inappropriate language or behavior and it must adhere to guidelines pertaining to intellectual property and plagiarism. You will often see videos running disclaimers at the beginning in order to be compliant with YouTube guidelines.

Also, it is worth noting that a channel may become eligible for AdSense monetization when it hits 1,000 subscribers and reaches 4,000 viewing hours. Once these two milestones have been hit, the channel is ready to apply for AdSense.

It should also be noted that just because a channel hits these marks it will automatically qualify. YouTube still reviews each application and will rule if the channel is suitable or not. This is often a long and painstaking process, but certainly worth the while, if achieved.

Tip #2: Sales funnel

YouTube channels are a great way of building a sales funnel.

In this tip, the channel is not producing income per se, but rather, it is engaging with viewers which can then turn into customers.

For instance, a channel may produce a series of how-to videos on home decoration. In this example, the channel itself is not producing any income. Income is produced when viewers click on a link provided and are redirected to a website where they can complete their purchase.

This is a classic example of how advertising is not about sales but rather building brand presence.

In addition, engaging viewers creates incoming traffic. As you may know, incoming traffic is highly convertible. Think of it this way, a person that walks into a store is much more likely to become a customer than a person who is standing on the street outside the store. The key is to get the person into the store. They will never make a purchase if they're just standing outside.

The same principle applies here. When viewers interact with the channel, they are similar to a person who walks into a store. As such, YouTube is a great way of directing traffic to your sales platform.

Tip #3: Affiliate marketing

Affiliate marketing has been touted as one of the best ways in which individuals can generate income.

Traditionally, affiliate marketing was about advertising products and services through your own marketing efforts.

That concept still holds true. However, YouTube is able to augment affiliate marketing in such a way that channels can work in tandem with sponsor brands.

A classic example of this approach is how-to videos which utilize products from sponsors in order to demonstrate how something is done. This is not the case of "This video is brought to you by..." but rather, you are demonstrating how an action is done by using a specific product which you will present in your video. Other examples are tutorials (similar to how-to videos), unboxing, product reviews, or even critiques.

All of these types of videos place the center of attention on the product that is being advertised and direct viewers' attention toward these specific items.

Of course, this isn't free. Affiliate members generally get a cut from product sales conducted through their channel. So, if a viewer clicks on a link which then leads to a purchase, that channel will receive a commission.

This type of monetization is highly dependent on solid content and may not always generate substantial income. In some cases, the income generated may not cover the cost of producing the video. Nevertheless, successful affiliate marketers can clean up by generating greater visibility to a brand.

Tip #4: Brand sponsors

This seems like a no-brainer.

Brands will scour YouTube in an attempt to find influencers and channels which are as popular with their core customers. Often, this leads brands to approach YouTube celebrities and propose agreements in which these celebrities will endorse their products in some way.

In some cases, it might be something as simple as being seen wearing a specific brand or using some type of brand name product. Other times, successful channels will openly push products by encouraging their subscribers to check out a given sponsor's brand.

This type of monetization tends to be done on the fringes of YouTube. However, great care needs to be taken since openly pushing a brand or product may be deemed to be a violation of policies. As such, it pays to double-check guidelines in order to ensure that content posted does not infringe said guidelines in any way.

One very important aspect to consider with sponsors: Channels are required to openly disclose their relationship to that advertiser in such a way that viewers are warned that they are endorsing a sponsor. So, it pays to do your homework on this particular aspect.

Tip #5: Community Sponsors

One of the newest ways in which YouTube has allowed a channel to monetize is through enabling a "community sponsor" feature. This feature allows viewers to sponsor a channel by making a monthly payment.

What this enables subscribers to do is to become a VIP member of that channel. Perhaps viewers aren't as interested in that type of recognition as they are interested in supporting the channel. This is why you often see YouTubers exhorting their viewers to support their channel.

This type of monetization can certainly generate a significant stream of income to a channel. Also, while this is a relatively new feature, it certainly affords the opportunity for successful channels to generate enough revenue to keep them alive.

This type of income is subject to taxation. In general, channel owners receive 70% of their revenue after taxes. Sure, losing 30% to taxes is nothing to sneeze at, but it does provide another relevant source of income.

Tip #6: Capitalize on YouTube Red subscribers

YouTube Red subscribers pay a monthly fee in order to eliminate ads from their viewing experience.

Since this a premium service, these subscribers get the red-carpet treatment. Also, successful channels can also horn in on this.

Eligible channels can receive a commission based on the amount of time YouTube Red subscribers spend on that channel. The more time these subscribers spend on your channel, the higher the commission. In order to qualify, similar AdSense rules apply (1,000 subscribers and 4,000 viewing hours).

Granted, meeting these requirements is not easy and demand substantial time and effort. This is why having a clear strategy for your channel will enable you to create the type of content that your viewers will be interested in and will boost your following.

Tip #7: Actually, sell something

I know that I've talked about how marketing is not about selling, and I stand by that.

In this tip, my point is that your videos while delivering value to your subscribers, can openly sell your own products. You can make a point of asking viewers to visit your website or purchase your products on Amazon. Other channels offer paid subscription services to additional content not available on YouTube.

As such, you can be upfront about why you are doing what you are doing. Also, unlike affiliate marketing, you are not pushing someone else's products. Instead, you are drawing attention to your own products.

One such example is a book. Authors will often use YouTube to engage their target audience. They will provide free content as a platform to present their book. If the viewer is interested, they can visit the author's website or go to Amazon.

Therefore, your YouTube channel fulfills its main marketing purpose by becoming a vehicle by which you can advertise your own products directly to your core customers.

The tips are meant to give you a clear picture of the various possibilities of monetizing a YouTube channel. They all require time and dedication in order to achieve this purpose. When done right, channels can become highly profitable.

However, there are also potential pitfalls. That is why I would like to present the following lessons I have learned throughout my experience with monetizing channels.

Lesson #1: Having a clear strategy is absolutely necessary

When you don't have a clear strategy for your channel, successful monetization will be more dependent on luck than actual talent.

In addition to defining your channel's identity, it pays to have a clear idea of the following:

•Understand keywords

•Include a call to action

•Have clear scripts and descriptions

•Good quality recording

•Produce quality thumbnails

•Caption and schedule your video prior to publishing

These steps are vital to ensuring high-quality content. In particular, including the right keywords in your video's description will enhance its search engine optimization (SEO) and thereby make it easier for viewers to find it.

Lesson #2: SEO is the lifeline of a video

Since YouTube is a part of Google, SEO plays a vital role in making sure that your videos will come up in Google searches. By exploiting SEO, you can have a leg up on the competition.

SEO depends solely on keywords. Descriptions and captions rich on keywords will make your content visible to users on both Google searches and YouTube's algorithm. So, it pays to take the time to align your channel's content to SEO.

Lesson #3: Different audiences are engaged through different means

Often, content creators assume that audiences found on blogs and social media will automatically become interested in video content.

That isn't always the case.

You can't assume that because an individual reads your blog, they will automatically become interested in your video content.

The reverse is also true.

Your YouTube subscribers may not be interested in reading your blog or following you on social media. These are different media and should be treated as such.

That is why successful online marketing strategies offer different types of content throughout different platforms in order to give users a reason to follow you across various platforms. So, it's best to avoid assuming that users from one platform will crossover into another.

Lesson #4: Cross-promotion

In the lesson before, we underscored the importance of avoiding the assumption that users will automatically transfer from one platform to another.

Therefore, this implies that you must use on a platform as a springboard to another.

For example, YouTube offers a wonderful opportunity to share content which may not be practical on social media. In fact, social media may be utilized as a means of engaging customers in a completely different way. Social media might be used by your brand in order to generate sales but for sharing content.

This is why understanding the presence of your brand throughout various platforms will enable you to cross-promote effectively.

Let's consider this:

Your social media strategy may utilize short video clips to entice viewers to visit your YouTube channel. Conversely, your YouTube channel may redirect viewers to your sales platform. In this manner, you are integrating all available means of connecting with customers.

With online marketing, the name of the game is being present across various platforms in such a way that each platform represents a different facet of your brand.

YouTube as a marketing tool. At the end of the day, YouTube is just that, a tool.

YouTube is not the end-all and be-all of online marketing. It is just one of the many tools at your disposal. When you have a clear understanding of the role that YouTube plays in your brand strategy, you will be able to produce the type of content that will resonate with your subscribers and engage them across various platforms.

The most important takeaway is that building a successful channel is certainly within your reach. However, it requires a clearly defined strategy. That strategy begins with a keen understanding of your brand's philosophy and how YouTube can link your brand's philosophy with that of your customers.

HOW TO PROMOTE YOUR YOUTUBE CHANNEL

You have produced a video, or two, and a company to market and sell, but the research has just started in many respects. You'll need a plan to make sure that people other than your family and friends see your film. You can't just post the video in the same manner and wait for people to come to you. When pushing the snowball down the hill, publicity plays a significant role.

How to promote

But the Web is mostly anonymous and massive. How do you spread the word about your work? How are you going to draw subscribers? What can you do to ensure your message gets to the target audience? The answers lie with the observations and perspectives of thousands of YouTube residents who have worked this out for themselves and were then happy to share with us what they have found.

Then, take a deep breath and note one thing: this is not brain surgery. You need to get that consumer to recognize it, give him or her something to consider, and present your case to someone to sell a product or service to. If you have made a good video, and you may be involved in targeting people, you know, you should find your audience. George Wright of Blendtec puts it this way, "You needn't be on YouTube's front page. You have to be on the front page wherever your audience is gathering. Isolate, find, and become involved in that corner of the Internet. "That's excellent advice, and we're about to give you plenty of ways to achieve this goal. But since making it to the front page of YouTube wouldn't hurt, we're going to cover that, too. The method of distributing the video across the Internet is named "seeding."

While describing the YouTube video marketing trend of the 21st century, the word seeding seems anachronistic. But if you want to be a star with YouTube, you'd best get used to it, whether you've got a green thumb or not. Once you've planted your videos correctly, you'll want to power them, too. Seeding is building momentum for your video, and it keeps driving running. "Our seedlers get the momentum going," clarified the Woo Agency's David Abehsera, "and our fueling remains on that. Right off the bat, our [Sean Kingston's Beautiful Girls] video went all over the place. "Over 46 million people had embraced Beautiful Girls when we last reviewed.

When it comes to the seeding, David Mullings is something of a Web, Johnny Appleseed. He also produced popular YouTube promotions that include celebrities such as Mariah Carey and Cezar, Coca-Cola's first-ever supported Reggae artist. David is only 27, but he's a veteran of YouTube with tried and tested online marketing techniques that he makes. David embeds his YouTube videos on his own Web site's front page. "I embed the video on Realvibeztv's front page," he explained. "We get over 1,000 visits to the site a day, and even though we could run the video in our player, it doesn't generate almost as much advertising as a hit on YouTube." David shared some of his favorite suggestions. Video Marketing Measures by David Mullings:

• Share the link on YouTube.

• Update your Facebook status (e.g., to claim you post a video).

• Tweet about it. • Send the connection to all interested people.

• Upload a select group of Facebook friends and invite them to post it on their pages.

• Post the video link in suitable groups.

• Post the link or embed the video on relevant message boards. And the secret sauce: • Upload the video into your Web site's front page. Through Facebook and Twitter, you can see that David uses any resource at his fingertips to insert video links, old-fashioned email marketing, and new techniques such as email blasts. First, let's take a look at the simple techniques. Like so many other projects, as we go, we'll start and develop to more complex and diverse approaches.

Some video promotion steps

There are many ways to get you started seeding your videos. Along the way, blogs, email blasts, even simple word of mouth, will be used. Ultimately, you're going to want people all over the Web to know about your work, but we want you to see how far you can go just by promoting your work on YouTube itself before you start spreading that word. There is a lot of work to do right there at first before you want to venture out all over the neighborhood.

Start on YouTube

YouTube provides plenty of ways to promote the content to ensure it reaches as many people as possible on the web. This part of the process is vitally important, as every month, over 200 million unique users visit the site. It's smart to optimize the visibility of your video right there.

Post frequently

It is essential to regularly post, particularly once you have started having a subscriber base. Your goal is to have fans in pursuit of your future photo. If you don't publish new work, the subscribers will ignore you and pass on to more regular contributors.

Hold it and encourage it with new work while you have their focus.

You must keep your share of the space of mind of your fans! Comedian Asa Thibodaux posts on YouTube, about four videos a week. "When you reach a certain level," he notes, "it's a compromise between the number of videos and the number of subscribers." (Asa has over 20,000 subscribers.) It's fascinating that Michael Buckley, of What the Buck?! Fame, he gave the same advice a lot. And He's got over 250,000 members! He says, "the trick for me now is quick video formation. I'm producing three to four videos a week. "For Michael, it's about" staying in touch with your friends, "so having videos posted is the best way to do that.

Use the Share Option

For a very brief time, your video gets its best exposure on YouTube — when it's just uploaded to the system. Clicking on a group connection (say News & Politics) helps audiences to zoom in on exciting videos by clicking on the hyperlinks above, like Featured, The Videos, and Most Mentioned. Nevertheless, if they press the down arrow beside the more button, Recent Videos can be viewed. That would be yours, for some time, at least.

You'll need to be more cautious after that. YouTube is one of the best tools for spreading your content right under your nose—or the nose of your user, that is. As people view it, it's the Sharing button that shows under your picture. Tap that, and one of the choices you'll get is to "submit this picture." You can either fill in the box with an e-mail address, or highlight All Contacts or Friends, and YouTube can e-mail it to the people on those lists. By the way, when they have accepted your invitation to do so, you become friends with other YouTubers. Those invitations are sent from your Channel page.

Pay attention to the comment

People can make whatever remarks about your videos they choose, as long as you allowed this option when you posted it. That's all right. The responses can be quite humorous; they can trigger more conversation and indicate how famous or controversial your video is.

Yet did you know that you are in charge of those comments? That is a good thing since feedback will work as effectively against you as they can work for you. "You have to look at the comments shared on your post," recommends Serena Software's Michael Parker. "With inappropriate remarks, keep an eye out." What is unacceptable?

Anything that is totally off track, such as spam directing people to a different video or link, something meaningless, or comments littered with curse words and typos. We warn against this so much as we appreciate the urge to delete the negative comments and leave positive ones. When supporters react to the negative comments, the conversation that can start can raise the scores. At the beginning of each of his episodes, as Michael Buckley states, "Rate it, even if you dislike it!" You will find all the assistance you need to manage your comments on the Help Center for YouTube.

Related Videos

It's all about getting more views, so you're seeding like a farmer if a thumbnail of your video appears as a related video. When your video covers the same territory as other videos, this happens. It then comes under the heading Similar Links at the right of those links. Which ensures you get more publicity! We want to advise you exactly how to make sure that your video for the site's most popular videos shows under Related Videos. Yet YouTube makes it clear that when the video appears as a Similar Post, you do not influence it. They're selected based on "multiple variables." YouTube states elsewhere on the web that similar videos are "picked through a complex search algorithm. They may be related to the video that you are watching!"(This is adorable but not all that helpful.) The style, logo, tags, and explanation of your video help to decide what other videos are connected to it. Therefore, take them out carefully. It's also to your benefit that if it's utterly unrelated to the one anyone sees; the footage doesn't qualify as a related video. Again, you don't want people to get annoyed.

Subscribers and YouTube community

Many of the advertising platforms that we will be talking about here all take us to the same thing— building a base of fans. Any star will tell you just how critical to their popularity a fan club can be. Your subscriber base on YouTube is one big fan group, one that you want to build and grow. Serving the fan club takes two steps: creating a subscription list and then engaging with that list.

Individuals posting on your posts are a fantastic source of potential subscribers. Fitzy advises that you "give them a message or hit them back on their MySpace or Twitter." In so doing, he notes, "means a lot to them." One way to get viewers is to query them: invite people to subscribe to your channel right on your Channel website.

Ultimately, it's the quality of your videos that builds your subscriber base above all else. Michael Buckley's got a knack to hit all the hot buttons on pop culture, and that's served him well. "I had 9,000 customers there a year ago," he told us. Then, "I was listed with LonelyGirl15 on YouTube front page is Dead! That has taken me about 7,000 subscribers. Many popular YouTubers have given me exposure. It has been a steady rise ever since. "Once you have a subscriber base, reaching out to them through platforms such as Instagram, then contacting them on your MySpace and Facebook pages helps to keep them linked. How relevant all of this depends on what kind of videos you're selling. Comedians like Michael Buckley and Asa Thibodaux are searching for tons of viewers–the stronger. This objective is less critical for Serena Software since it is the quality of the leads, they harvest that counts more than the sheer number of people who subscribe.

Measuring your views

The most critical measure is the number of views how many times the video has been downloaded. This number appears on the video page, directly below the video player.

How many views is a good number when it comes to judging the simple performance?

That's tough to say. Of course, if your video receives one million views immediately, you're doing the right thing — that's a total viral celebrity. Nevertheless, a minimum of 100 views might be perfect for certain types of videos and businesses. (For starters, if you're selling high-priced real estate.) You've got to assess performance based on your criteria and with realistic expectations. Just because the video has a lot of viewers doesn't imply it has reached the aims you set out to accomplish. A video of 100,000 views is excellent, but if you wanted to boost your revenue, it doesn't mean much. Entertaining viewers on YouTube is one thing; generating sales (or creating a brand image or anything else) is quite another. Using a thumbs up / thumbs down system, viewers can rate a video–up if they like it, down if not.

Tracking its effectiveness and interactivity

The number of impressions that a video receives don't automatically mean how successful it is. A video may attract a large audience but result in little sales or brand awareness; conversely, a video with a limited number of viewers may result in much higher sales or brand awareness.

Measuring a video's success is harder than merely measuring the audience.

No analytical instruments measure this metric; it is more of a black art than a science. There are ways to get a general handle over how useful a video is with that caveat. Another indicator of effectiveness is how well the audiences are engaged with the film — that is, how viewers communicate with the content. You can reduce the level of engagement from the number of comments made by the viewers and video replies. The more the video pulls in audiences, the more people can leave personal messages and questions.

Speak of it like this. If your video is just light entertainment, it certainly won't inspire people to leave comments. If your picture, on the other side, is particularly useful or informative, viewers are more likely to leave feedback to this impact.

The more feedback you receive, the more the audience gets engaged with the film.

On a meta-level, you can measure the success of all of your videos in total by seeing how many subscribers you get to your YouTube channel! If your videos communicate with audiences, they are more likely to subscribe to your channel for future video feedback. If your videos are less effective, the viewers are less likely to sign up.

Traffic and conversion

If you are using your YouTube videos to market products or services directly from your page, actually monitoring traffic from each YouTube video back to your platform is the best way to measure the success of each post. There's a lot of ways to do that. Just about any website analytics tool will show where your site traffic originates—that is, the past sites viewed by visitors to your site. By using this sort of method, the traffic from the YouTube site to your domain is easy enough to monitor. If you see an increase in YouTube traffic after posting a new video, it's a good bet that this video had driven the traffic.

More advanced monitoring software for the website monitors traffic from specific pages on the originating platform. This makes the decision of which videos bring the most traffic back to your platform much better.

Instead, each video you post to YouTube can include a unique code.

The easiest way to do that is to show in each YouTube video a specific URL for your main site; the URL will connect to a special landing page on your website. Another way to measure success with video is to determine what type of response you want. Is the video designed to generate direct sales either through your website or through your 800-number? Is that video meant to drive traffic to your website? Is the video designed to enhance or reinforce your reputation as an organization or brand? Or is the video designed to cut the cost of customer support or technical support?

This is key — to measure your YouTube video's success, you must first determine what you're hoping to achieve. Then you can calculate the results, and only then:

• If you aim to generate sales, then evaluate sales. Include in the video your website URL and 800-number, along with a coupon or order code, and then monitor purchases, which include that code.

• If your goal is to drive traffic to your website, then calculate your pre-and post-YouTube traffic footage. Using web monitoring to determine the source of site traffic, explicitly monitor the traffic coming straight from the YouTube site.

• Measurement is more complicated if your goal is to create your brand image.

Once the YouTube promotion has had a chance to do its thing, you'll need to do some market research and ask customers what they think of your brand — and where they learned about it.

• If your goal is to the consumer or technical support expenses, measure the number of requests for assistance before and after posting the video(s) on YouTube. The more successful the picture, the less supportive the corresponding calls

YOUTUBE ADVERTISING

Advertising on YouTube is a serious endeavor. If done right, you can generate quite a large number of conversions, build up brand awareness and even help promote your own channel. However, YouTube advertising is no small expense. While the cost of running the ads can vary, there are initial costs associated with creating the YouTube ad itself. However, since a YouTube video ad is essentially a commercial, we won't be covering how to make one. Instead, we'll be discussing how YouTube advertising works, how you can get the most out of your advertising dollar and the different types of YouTube ads available.

AdWords

Since YouTube is owned by Google, you're going to need what's known as a Google AdWords account. AdWords is their advertising system that allows for you to advertise through Google's search engine. Outside of video ads, AdWords is a paid advertising service that will put your website links first after specific searches are made in Google.

Creating an advertising account with Google is fairly simple. Once you do that, you'll need to link your YouTube channel to the account. This will allow for you to select which videos you want to be shown when running an ad.

Ad Types:

YouTube has a few different types of advertisements available for you to utilize. These all have different costs and benefits, depending on what your goals are.

TrueView

TrueView ads are created with both the advertiser and the consumer in mind. There are two different classes of TrueView ads, In-Stream and Video Discovery. A TrueView In-Stream video ad can run for as long as you like, but consumers always have the option to skip after the first five seconds. If the viewer skips before 30 seconds are up, you aren't charged for the ad spot.

The value behind this is that you won't end up boring customers or consumers who aren't interested in your product. And, since you can run your ad for as long as you like, a consumer who is interested in what you have to say will be more than willing to sit and watch the entire thing. This really is a win-win situation when it comes to advertising.

The second type of TrueView ad is known as Video Discovery. Video Discovery simply means that your video is placed in key locations on YouTube, usually at the top of the recommended videos or in the search. This simply sticks your video up at the top and allows for consumers who are interested to click on it and watch your ad. You are charged, however, every time a viewer clicks on that ad, regardless of how long they watch it.

Unskippable Ads:

If you'd prefer that your viewers see the entirety of your ad, without the option to skip, then you'll need to simply use either the pre-roll or mid-roll ad option. Pre-roll is an ad that is placed at the very beginning of the video and mid-roll ads will show up in the middle. Both are unskippable and have a maximum time of 20 seconds. However, times are paring down somewhat, and 15 seconds is becoming the norm in terms of unskippable ads.

The cost for pre or midroll ads is what's known as CPM or cost-per-mille, meaning for every 1,000 views, you are charged. The rates, of course, vary based on a number of factors, including the ad space that you are targeting, the number of advertisers who are trying to move into the same space and the number of viewers who usually watch the types of video you are advertising in front of.

Bumper Ads:

A bumper is an extremely short ad, lasting to a maximum of 6 seconds. They are unskippable, just like pre and midroll, and they have the same fee structure. The big question would be, why use a bumper ad? Six seconds might seem very short, but the purpose of a bumper ad isn't to outright call for action. Rather that short of a time will increase what's known as ad recall lift. Ad recall lift represents how many people will remember your advertisement within a period of two days. By running small, quick bumper ads in conjunction with a larger advertising campaign, you have a greater chance of helping customers remember your ads. And if they remember your ads, they may end up deciding to check it out after a while.

Another valuable asset that bumper ads bring is the fact that they are short. Most consumers these days don't particularly enjoy ads and would much rather get through them as quickly as possible. By having these short, six second ads, you can tell your viewers about your product or promotion quickly, without having to worry about them becoming annoyed by your ad length. It's quick, effective and will help them remember you.

Targeted Advertising:

Once you have a general idea about the type of ad that you want to run, you'll need to make sure that you have all the data necessary for targeted advertising. Fortunately, Google's advertising systems are quite powerful, able to get your ads in front of the most relevant audience possible, provided that you have the right data for them.

The first and most important type of data to use is the right keywords. You may have a general idea of what kind of product you're going to advertise, but you'll need the right and most relevant keywords possible if you want to put your ad in front of the right people. Google has a keyword planner tool that you can use when setting up your ad. This planner will help you shape which keywords you want to target. You'll be able to see which keywords and phrases are being searched for on Google and which ones are the most relevant to your target audience. In general, you'll want to select keywords that are being searched often and by a large amount of people. This will maximize your chances of exposure, since you'll be tapping into an extremely relevant group of people.

The other types of data that you can use for YouTube Advertising involves demographics, user interests, life events and purchasing decisions. Google offers a tremendous amount of options and they are, for the most part, self-explanatory. This is one of the most important aspects of advertising, of course. The better you are able to target your audience, the more relevant your ads are and that translates to generating higher levels of conversion. Take your time and don't rush through these sections. Do everything in your power to fill out as much of these options as possible, so you have a wide, relevant audience to put your ads in front of.

Video Remarketing:

Google is able to keep track of its user viewing habits. As such, they are able to directly target people who have watched your videos or are subscribed to your channel. This practice is known as video remarketing and it is similar to Facebook's retargeting. Remarketing allows for you to create lists based on the type of viewer that you want to target. For example, if you've been doing a series about Product A, and you have 2,000 views of that product, you can create a list out of those viewers. Then, when you run your advertisement, you can place the ad right in front of those viewers.

Remarketing is an extremely effective way to sell your products, primarily since you already know that they have demonstrated some level of interest in what you are selling. They are considered to be warm leads and as such, will most likely respond positively to your ads.

On top of that, you can also use remarketing to further hone the efficiency of the video ads after they have finished a run. If your video was displayed in front of 3,000 people, you can retarget those same 3,000 viewers. This is exceptionally useful when it comes to using TrueView ads, which only count a view if a consumer watches the video for thirty seconds, or until the video ends, whichever is shorter.

Since TrueView ads are opt-in, meaning customers choose to sit and watch them, they are already warmer leads than those who chose not to watch the ad at all. You can select a different, more targeted video ad to run in front of these people who have already expressed interest. This will generate a much higher return on investment.

Evaluating Analytics:

Just like with Facebook ads, running ads on YouTube is all about analytics. Once you've run a few ad campaigns, you'll have the numbers to be able to determine the efficiency of your ad campaigns. From there, you'll then have to evaluate the data and determine which ads are worth keeping, which ads are underperforming, and which ones should be reworked. Remember, when you're just starting out with advertising campaigns, you shouldn't be discouraged if you aren't seeing stellar results right out of the gate. Advertising campaigns take time to fine tune, but each time you run them, as long as you are willing to work with the data you receive, you'll be able to improve them over time. Combined with a solid video remarketing strategy, you'll be able to increase your conversion rates in no time!

USING SOCIAL MEDIA TO PROMOTE YOUR CHANNEL

The primary goal of using social media is only to increase your view count in your videos and develop a strong fan base that favors your videos. This doesn't directly give you any profits, but it helps build a solid viewer base and reaches out to those who do not know about you or your videos. In the end, it all comes down to your view count and ad clicks on your videos, which significantly affects your profit.

If used in the right way, social media can help boost your view count several folds. As mentioned before, your YouTube videos have their unique address or "URL." Copy this URL and paste it in your Facebook, Twitter, or any forums you frequent. Any user who clicks this URL will be directed to your YouTube video, at which point, if it interests the person, he will subscribe and add to your pool of views. Make sure to include these URLs only in places that do disturb or annoy the other users.

Try and convince your family and friends to see your videos beforehand when you start out. It is important to get someone's opinion as it may be different from yours. Try to correct your mistakes before using social media platforms to promote your videos and channel. If you end up uploading a mediocre video in your initial stages, your audience will get an impression of you being a mediocre video creator. Under no circumstances should this happen. So, take precautionary measures, and make your first few videos the best before promoting them.

Given below are some of the most widely used social media platforms to effectively promote your videos and channel. Read on to know how you should go about promoting your videos and how you can gain a larger audience.

Facebook

Facebook, as an example, is the perfect place to paste these URLs on your own timeline or on a Facebook page that you have created to promote your channel. This way, only people who are interested can view your videos. Unnecessarily posting URLs and videos on another user's page or private chats could take a turn for the worse as it builds a bad reputation. Facebook has the additional option of paid marketing. You pay a nominal price, and your videos will be displayed at the top of the user's homepage. This means more traffic as your videos have more chance of being watched if they are placed first. Despite nominal prices, you might not want to use this option initially until you have enough subscribers and a steady view count. Using YouTube for profit requires zero initial investment, and hence, you should be able to pay for the marketing from your profits and not your pockets.

Despite this, many viewers stop watching your videos after clicking on your link. To overcome this, link the URL of a playlist of your videos that are related in some way or the other instead of a single video. This helps the viewers get interested and stay interested.

Instagram

Not many YouTube video creators consider using Instagram as a way to promote their videos, but it is an absolute fun and easy way to do so. As with Facebook and Twitter, you need to link your Instagram account as well on your YouTube channel and vice-versa. Instagram should be used to give regular updates about your life if you want to, of course. Most people like to know about the daily life of YouTubers, and you should get a good number of hits on your Instagram profile, which means you also have a chance at gaining more hits on your YouTube channel and videos. Apart from this, you can and should upload teasers of your future video. It should not contain the essence of the video itself; instead, you need to post pictures that make the audience hungry for more. This way, you are guaranteed a good number of views on your videos if you make your Instagram posts enigmatic. A good idea would be to release a teaser the day before you upload the actual video. This ensures your viewers are still interested. Setting up an Instagram account is relatively easy, and you can update your posts on it regularly with just your smartphone, which saves a lot of time.

Twitter

Twitter also holds great potential in increasing your view count. Hashtags are your greatest weapons; use them right, and you can easily set a trend that helps with promoting your video. Make sure to reach out to people with similar interests as you and give them shootouts in your videos and request them to do the same for you. This ensures that their fans, subscribers, and viewers know about you, which once again spells nothing but profit.

Being interactive is one of the best ways to sustain the interests of your viewers, and Twitter chat is the best way to interact with your viewers. Create a custom hashtag, tell your viewers the exact date and time you will be online to chat, and start chatting! Interact with your viewers, respond to questions, figure out what they expect more from you, build some trust, and lastly, always thank them for spending their precious time to view your videos. This not only helps create more interest but also a higher number of viewers as everybody likes their opinion being considered. This can sound slightly arduous and time-consuming, but Twitter is very smartphone friendly. You can perform these actions while traveling or when you have free time, saving you time that can be used to create content for your future video or to go about your daily life. While Facebook should be the primary platform through which you get the support of viewers, you should aim to provide regular updates on the topic of the upcoming video via Twitter. Note that your tweet is limited to 140 characters, so it only makes sense to keep your updates as short and mysterious as possible to provoke the interests of your viewers. Always link URLs to your videos at the end of your Facebook post or Twitter tweet.

Blogs

If you are a blogger with an already well-established audience, promoting your YouTube channel should be much easier. Simply include URLs to your blog on your YouTube channels and to your YouTube channel in your blog. This leads to more traffic in both places and hence more income. Creating videos related to the article you blogged about and pasting their URLs in your article is the best way to increase traffic. A video demonstration or tutorial or summary is always preferred to a written one. A blog requires you to regularly update the content; else it loses the interest of viewers. This gives an incentive to update your YouTube videos and stay ahead of others in trending topics to tremendously support your blog and vice-versa.

If you are not interested in creating a blog and maintaining it or feel that it takes up too much of your time, then it is a good idea to look up bloggers who create similar content to your videos. You can then request them to link your videos or your channel in their blogs for a small fee (only if the blogger has a large fan base, of course) or you could strike a deal where you link their blogs in your videos and they link your videos in their blogs. This is a great way to set up mutual trust and gain each other's followers.

Google+

YouTube is owned by Google, so why not use Google's own social media platform, Google+, to promote your channel? The great thing about Google+ is that you don't have a character limit like Twitter does. It is a great replacement for blogging, and you should consider it as a miniature blogging platform. All you need to do is create your own personal logo, a custom look on the channel, and give your Google+ page a personal touch to let yourself be more easily recognizable. You can include your video links in your posts to gain more support. Unlike Facebook, a large number of Google+ users use it for marketing. You should try to find out similar individuals or professionals in the same niche and engage with them. Try to share their posts if you feel the need to do so, and you increase your chances of them sharing your content. It is also a great place to get feedback and advice from professionals who have already been down the road you are taking. Like Twitter, hashtags are used in Google+ as well, but just not to the same extent. Use precise hashtags to get more hits and never give your posts innumerable inaccurate hashtags as it is an indisputable way of bringing forth hate comments from your audience.

MySpace

MySpace is another popular social networking website and can be used extensively to promote your YouTube channel.

The Share Trend

Sharing is an amazing way to rally more viewers. All it requires is you to ask your viewers to share your videos if they liked it with their friends and family. It is a given that most of them won't. But once a few people start sharing and your videos get around, it's only a matter of time before it is trending.

The idea behind sharing is to get you introduced to people who do not know about your videos yet. They view your videos and, in turn, share them, which leads to a hopefully never-ending cycle. Shares are the best way to get your videos around. What this means is your videos gain more traffic.

A requirement to this is a lenient privacy setting on your social media pages like Facebook and Twitter. You want your videos to be watched by people other than your friends. Make sure your videos are visible to the public at large, and you have a shot at gaining the large number of viewers that you want. Keeping your settings secured eventually will lead to a loss in your subscriber count as your videos will not be going around the social media platform as much as you would like them to. For this reason, it is optimal to create a different account or a page in the social media platform dedicated only to your videos. You can link back to your personal profile which you will be keeping secure and tell your viewers to personally give you requests and feedback 0r so there. This helps with security as well as getting you the maximum shares possible.

Social media is all about a person's opinion being heard. You may upload videos and promote them with all your resources, and they will not generate the expected traffic if you do not take some time to respond to your viewers. This is the most important part of using social media to promote videos. Always remember to ask people to like, subscribe, and comment. This will give you a general feedback. Ignore the mean posts if they do not have any constructive criticism. A good idea would be to upload a "Q & A" video where you answer some of the questions asked in your previously uploaded videos. This serves a dual role of making your viewers feel appreciated and increasing your income.

Effectively utilizing the social media available to you almost guarantees in gaining never-before-seen traffic and subscribers. It also ensures you have active and not passive subscribers, i.e., those who subscribe to you and view your videos regularly.

ANALYZE AND ADAPT

The worst thing you can do is just take that information and file it away. That would serve no purpose even if all you get are glowing reviews about how great your content is. In fact, if your content does get rave reviews, you might want to take an even deeper look at where you might be faltering especially because your competition won't let you off the hook so easily.

When everything is roses, it's easy to relax and even become complacent. If you do become complacent, you are only asking for trouble. The fact is that your social media marketing strategy needs to be in constant evolution along with the changes in the behavioral patterns of your customers, viewers, and subscribers.

However, when you don't get such positive feedback and reviews, you need to decide on what direction your content will take. Sure, it's true that not all content performs in the same manner. Nonetheless, when you can observe a trend, then you need to do something about it.

If you begin to observe a negative trend, then you would need to address it as soon as possible in order for you to turn the ship around and get your metrics back on track.

What to do when everything is going well

When you have developed a strong following and you have cooked up a successful formula, you need to focus on which aspects you could improve in order to keep your followers coming back and how you can ensure that new subscribers will keep coming.

Often, when you have devised a positive formula, it is tempting to stick to it until the cows come home. However, overdoing a formula will eventually kill your momentum.

So, what do you do?

Well, the answer lies in determining what makes your content click with your users.

For example, if your brand has developed characters which resonate with your core customers, then you might be tempted to ride those characters as long as possible. However, there has to come to a point where customers simply get tired of the same content. So, you would need to find the best way to phase out one character and bring a new one in.

The use of characters is just one way in which we can exemplify how there is a need for freshening up content every once in a while. Even if you have a successful formula, you need to experiment with other things so that your content is fresh and keeps viewers interested in what you have to offer.

The same goes for ads.

Even the most successful ad campaign in history wore off to a point where advertisers had to come up with something new in order to keep their customers interested and engaged with the brand.

A common example of this is how brands redesign their corporate logo. Successful multinational brands tend to spice up their logos at a 10-year tempo. The reason for this is due to the fact that generations of customers tend to turn over every decade.

Think about it.

You change quite a bit as a person in 10 years. That is why brands need to change at a similar tempo.

For brands which engage younger demographics, they may need to turn over their corporate image at an even quicker tempo since younger demographics demand change and innovation.

Therefore, feedback becomes a vital tool in determining if your brand needs an adjustment, and most importantly, what kind of an adjustment.

What about when things don't go well?

Now, let's assume that things aren't going too well.

This is when you need to listen the most. Your customers will be happy to tell you what you are doing wrong especially if they have been your customers for a while. Perhaps you made some changes that didn't sit well with your followers.

Perhaps you introduced products that didn't work out too well. Or, you might have even decided to cut certain things from your value proposition. Other times, there is content that just doesn't work out.

In any event, your customers will be the first to tell you why things aren't working out. You don't need to pay high-priced consultants. You can just ask your customers. However, you must be ready to hear what they have to say... and it might not be pretty.

Still, if you do actually pay attention, then you will certainly have a lot of information which you can use to adjust your strategies.

A good rule of thumb to follow is the rule of three. If you hear the same thing from at least three different customers that you are sure to have no way of communicating with each other, then you can be sure that something is up with your products, service, or just overall marketing efforts.

So, if things aren't going well, it shouldn't be a cause for frustration. It should be a good opportunity to promote change and allow these negative experiences to serve as lessons learned for future marketing efforts.

Lessons learned

On the subject of lessons learned, your mistakes can feed your collection of lessons learned.

What does that mean?

Well, it means that whatever you choose to do, if it doesn't go well, you must learn why it didn't go well and take note of why it didn't happen the way you expected it to. What you learn from these circumstances will feed your experience.

Bear in mind that you can learn a lot more from what goes wrong than from what goes right.

I recall one piece of advice that a mechanic once gave me, "you can learn a lot more when a car breaks down than when it doesn't".

Those are some of the wisest words I have learned in my life.

If you try your best to make a car breakdown a learning experience, you will learn so much more on the proper way a car should run. That way, you will be able to make sure that your car keeps running well all the time.

This metaphor serves to illustrate how you should rest on your laurels when things are going well. Also, it serves to illustrate how you should take every negative experience as an opportunity to learn something new about your brand, your products, your customers, and yourself.

At the end of the day, the worst thing you can do is take failure as such and give up. When you give up, the game is over.

The need for innovation

Seasoned veterans in the business world will tell you that innovation is necessary for all aspects of life. You can't expect your brand and your business to grow without innovation.

Innovation is a vital component to improving your current processes, value proposition, and even products themselves.

How can you determine where you can improve and innovate?

Simply ask your customers.

Even if everything is perfect, you can always ask them what you can do to improve what you are doing.

Customers will be happy to tell you where you are hitting it out of the park and where you can fine-tune things to make your business machine run well.

Innovation is the antidote to complacency. When you are committed to innovating, you are committed to becoming better each day. While that doesn't mean that you will not celebrate when things are going well, you should keep in mind that there is always something you can do better.

Think of sports teams.

Even when a sports team is riding high, good coaches will point out mistakes in their game and find the ways to address those areas. Perhaps one area is so good that it makes up the other areas.

For instance, a highly effective offensive team can make up for the defensive shortcoming. Or, a team is so good defensively that makes up for their lack of offense.

Whatever the case, good coaches will try their best to shore up the weak links. In most cases, it's just a matter of time before really good opponents expose a team's weaknesses and make them look bad when it counts.

CONCLUSION

Marketing businesses have never been this easy with the advent of the Internet. Businesspersons not only find it convenient to market their brands over the Internet, but they also find it affordable. YouTube is one of the leading social media pages out there. With millions of people accessing it on a daily basis, it means that it stands as a great platform to market your brand. Just like Facebook, people expect to communicate with brands in a natural way. Therefore, the marketing strategies that you employ will make a difference in your campaign. Unique marketing strategies that you use will definitely make you a loveable brand among your audience.

One of the most important considerations that should be remembered is the fact that the message is very important. What you tell your audience about your product or service will give them an overall picture of your brand. Crafting the right message will, therefore, have a positive impact on your audience. As had been recommended, you need to keep it short. Your message should also be clear. If your audience cannot figure out exactly what you are selling, then you need to redraft your message again.

With regards to improving your video quality, it also begins by working on your content. Besides this, you should take the time to learn more about the essentials required in producing great videos. For instance, if you lack the experience in shooting videos, you can always turn to an expert for assistance. They have the experience that will transform your idea into a must-watch type of video. Equally, you need to invest in purchasing the right equipment that will get you the results you need.

Think outside the box when it comes to creating your YouTube video. Think about the expectations that your customers have in mind. Create videos that not only meet their expectations but surpass them. You need your clients to keep coming to your YouTube channel. This implies that you have to captivate them with your content. The strategies should help you in becoming a good marketer on YouTube.

Another thing worth recalling is the fact that there are various ways to use YouTube for your business. Before rushing in to use YouTube to promote your business, you should first consider why it is important for your business. For instance, the platform could be used to market specific products and services that you offer. Alternatively, it could also be used in promoting your company in general. Your YouTube use will have an impact on the marketing strategies that you would adopt. Hence, the purpose of YouTube should be carefully determined at the early stages of your marketing campaign.

Most importantly, you need to evaluate how your YouTube marketing strategy is working out. This calls for the use of YouTube analytic tools. These tools will help you gauge the effectiveness of the videos that you upload. For instance, the subscriber rate will give you an insight into whether the content resonates with your audience or not. A higher subscriber rate implies that your audiences love your videos. On the contrary, a low subscriber rate will mean that your content needs some adjustment. Consequently, you should resort back to the tips that will help you in improving your video content.

Equally, there are specific things that you should not forget about when marketing your brand on YouTube. These essentials will determine whether or not your marketing efforts will pay off. For instance, a simple mistake like forgetting to post regularly will destroy your online presence. As a YouTube marketer, you need to embrace the idea of having evergreen content on your channel. Your customers need access to content that is always fresh. If you must post videos that are outdated, edit them and update them where necessary. Also, you need to understand that there are other things that you should not be doing on YouTube. Keeping your channel private, for example, is a huge mistake. It will cost you the entire marketing campaign. You will realize it when it is too late, and your competitors have pushed you out of the industry.

It should also come to your attention that your followers have other social media pages that they often use. This implies that you need to have an online presence on those pages where your prospects are active. Post your YouTube videos here and market them appropriately. The fact that you are uploading content to your YouTube channel doesn't mean that you are limited. Focus on getting your promotional message to as many social pages. In the end, you will increase your reach.

All things considered, there are various companies using YouTube to market their businesses. Standing out from these companies simply requires that you adopt the recommended marketing strategies mentioned in this material. The interesting thing is that there is nothing out of the ordinary that you need to understand. The issues covered are basically marketing tactics that you might have been aware of. You should pay attention to the essentials as they will determine the success or failure of your YouTube marketing campaign.

Good Luck!